COAST

TO

COAST

RECENT AUSTRALIAN PROSE WRITING

COAST TO COAST

Selected by
KERRYN GOLDSWORTHY

ANGUS & ROBERTSON PUBLISHERS

ANGUS & ROBERTSON PUBLISHERS

Unit 4, Eden Park, 31 Waterloo Road,
North Ryde, NSW, Australia 2113, and
16 Golden Square, London W1R 4BN,
United Kingdom

First published in Australia
by Angus & Robertson Publishers in 1986
First published in the United Kingdom
by Angus & Robertson UK in 1986

National Library of Australia
Cataloguing-in-publication data.

Coast to coast.

ISBN 0 207 15300 0.

1. Australian prose literature — 20th century. I. Goldsworthy, Kerryn, 1953-

A828'.30808

Typeset in English Times
Printed in Australia by The Book Printer

ACKNOWLEDGEMENTS

cknowledgements for permission to print these stories are ıe to the following:

Rosaleen Love for "The Laws of Life", published in *Westerly*, No 1, March 1985; Barry Westburg for "In the Maize", published in *Quadrant* No 219 Vol. XXX, Nos 1 & 2, January–February 1986; to be published in his short story collection *Tear Gas* (Angus & Robertson Publishers, 1987); Rosa Safransky for "Postcards", from *inprint*, Vol. 7, No 4, 1983; Glenda Adams for "The Voyage of Their Life", copyright Glenda Adams 1985, published in *Meanjin* Vol. 44 No 2, 1985, and *Triquarterly* 62, Winter 1985; to be published as part of the novel *Dancing on Coral* (Viking/Penguin, USA, 1987 and Angus & Robertson Publishers, 1987); Viking/Penguin for Frank Moorhouse's "Cultural Delegate" from *Room Service* (1985); Don Watson for "Gd Ship Country", published under the title "A Land Purely Beautiful" in *The Age Saturday Extra*, 2/11/85; Penguin for excerpt from Vincent Buckley's *Memory Ireland* (1985); Penguin for excerpt from Bernard Smith's *The Boy Adeodatus* (1984); Anna-Maria Dell'oso for "The Softening of Blows", published under the title "How Godmothers Soften the Blow" in the *Sydney Morning Herald Good Weekend*, 23/11/85; Tim Winton for "Gravity", published in *Matilda* No 9, December 1985–January 1986; McPhee Gribble for Barry Hill's "Headlocks" (first published in *Overland*) from *Headlocks and Other Stories* (1983); Chatto & Windus for David Malouf's "The Kyogle Line" from *12 Edmondstone Street* (1985); Penguin for Gerard Windsor's "My Father's

Version of the Nurses' Story'' (first published in *Meanjin*, No 2, 1985) from *Memories of the Assasination Attempt and Other Stories* (1985); UQP for Olga Masters' ''The Christmas Parcel'' from *A Long Time Dying* (1985); Allen & Unwin Australia for excerpt from Kate Grenville's *Lilian's Story* (1985); Marian Eldridge for ''Primavera'', published in *Southerly*, No 1, 1985; subsequently published in *Best Short Stories 1986* (Heinemann, UK, 1986); Barbara Hanrahan for ''Ida Spider''; Suzanne Falkiner for ''My Grandmother the Sociologist''; Patrick Rogers for ''The Small Steel Box''; John Clanchy for ''The Art of Writing Dangerously''; Thomas Shapcott for ''The Competition Portrait''; Brian Dibble for ''If I Ever Decide To Im-mo-late Myself . . .'', published in *inprint*, II, July 1978; UQP for excerpt from Elizabeth Jolley's *Foxybaby* (1985); McPhee Gribble for Helen Garner's ''The Life of Art'' (first published in the *Australian*, 6–7/7/1985) from *Postcards from Surfers* (1985).

INTRODUCTION

It's not possible any more — if it ever was — to put together a collection of Australian writing which contains everything you would have liked it to contain. Had I done that, *Coast to Coast* would have run to three fat volumes at least. And these days there are so many good collections of Australian writing to be had that any given writer not represented in one is very likely to be found in another. The writing collected here consists not so much of the things I would have liked to put in as of the things I couldn't bear to leave out.

My brief as editor was to look for 'prose writing' rather than specifically 'short stories', a departure from *Coast to Coast* tradition which I found liberating and exciting not least because that made it possible to include writers of the calibre of, and as different as, Don Watson, Bernard Smith and Vincent Buckley. It also increased my conviction, as I chose and assembled the contents, that the distinction between fiction and non-fiction is a highly unstable one, something I have tried to demonstrate by the choice and juxtaposition of the pieces in this book.

They have, however, been ordered as they appear here for other reasons as well. As I gathered material for this book I was startled again and again by the number of items which seemed not so much to resemble each other as to speak to each other, to have in common ideas and preoccupations which, while manifesting themselves in different ways, seemed to form part of some dialogue or debate. So, rather than order the contents at random or chronologically or under a set of 'theme and subject' headings, I have tried to do something else. In Gerald Murnane's *Landscape With*

Landscape each of the stories departs from some point — a name, a phrase — in the last; the overall effect is that of one long narrative which takes strange dogleg turns from time to time but is essentially an unbroken line. And that is what I have tried to do here.

So the best way to read this book is to follow the advice of Alice's Red King: '"Begin at the beginning," said the King, very gravely. "Go on till you reach the end; then stop."' You may of course not want to stop at the end; I think the first story has something to say to the last, and I think all of these pieces are worth reading twice, at least. In ordering them I have tried to create the effect of lining up the authors in a circle and asking them to speak in turn, each taking her or his cue from something the previous speaker has said; I have tried to make each piece illuminate the others, lest something beautiful in the dark corners of narrative go otherwise unnoticed.

It is up to readers, really, to make their own connections, and it's entirely possible that some of these connections are visible only to me. But I hope that readers will gain something by seeing, say, Vincent Buckley and Bernard Smith engaged side by side in autobiographical acts which explore the nature of personal and national origins; or hearing Tim Winton, Barry Hill, David Malouf, Gerard Windsor, Olga Masters and Kate Grenville converse on the subject of fathers; or seeing Patrick Rogers, John Clanchy, Thomas Shapcott, Brian Dibble, Elizabeth Jolley and Helen Garner all wrestling with the nature of representation, especially representation of the human self, in painting or writing. Other connections are more casual or chancy, like a taxi that happens to pull up just as you get off the train. But they are, like the taxi, there.

I did not, however, choose the different items in order to fit this structure. I have left out three or four stories I particularly wanted to put in, but I have not put in anything I would otherwise have left out. There were, in choosing the contents, some measurable limits. 'Recent' writing has been defined as 'written or published within the last two or three years'. Anything too long would have denied space to other writers, which is the only reason why there is nothing here from Murnane's *Landscape With Landscape* or Eric Rolls' *Celebration of the Senses*, from neither of which it was possible to extract a passage that was both suitably self-contained and acceptably short.

Otherwise my criteria for choice were the only ones an editor can use: the nature and strength of personal responses to the writing. Some of these pieces are here not least because they either made me laugh aloud (Barry Westburg's 'In the Maize', Don Watson's 'Gd Ship Country', John Clanchy's 'The Art of Writing Dangerously') or shed actual wet tears (Gerard Windsor's 'My Father's Version of the Nurses' Story', Olga Masters' 'The Christmas Parcel', Helen Garner's 'The Life of Art'). Others, like the pieces by Anna-Maria Dell'oso or, again, Don Watson, appeared originally in the weekend papers and produced 'Did you read . . .?' conversations all round me for a week afterwards. Since this collection makes no claim at all to be 'representative' — as Don Anderson has said, 'representative of what?' — I have perhaps culpably made no conscious effort to include writing by members of various different special-interest or minority groups, so it is honestly fortuitous, if personally delightful to me, that eleven of the twenty-four pieces here are by women.

If all the items in this book have one thing in common, it is that each on first reading has stuck in my mind like a grain of sand in an oyster, leaving little pearly spots all over the inside shell of memory. Selecting and stringing them together for a revived *Coast to Coast* has been both a privilege and a rather demanding form of fun; all I can do now is hope that the writers and their readers like the pattern.

Kerryn Goldsworthy

Contents

Rosaleen Love

THE LAWS OF LIFE

They say that all life is one, that we have a common origin with animals, with plants, with bacterial sludge even. This common root in the tree of life has given some of the young of the human species a special kind of sympathy. We are born into a knowledge of what is going on in the living world. We have an intuitive grasp of the language of life. I had this gift, and it was what made me try for a career in science. I thought it would be a pushover. I was, of course, ever mindful of the words of the song:

I talk to the trees
That's why they put me away.

So I kept my talent a secret. But no one can be certain of anything in the present job situation, and this is the sad story of my career.

I had a tough time to begin with. It was as hard for me, as for anyone else, to understand the structure of cells or the embryonic development of the frog. At this level, my gift counted for nothing. I couldn't ask a pine tree intimate details about its mode of sexual reproduction. It's very vague about the details. All that comes through is the sense that every now and then an overwhelming urge comes over it, and staminate cones sprout on one branch, and ovulate cones on another. It knows nothing of pollination and cross-fertilisation. It's like asking a politician, what is the good life? Useless. Plants are too busy photosynthesising to be self-reflexive, and that's why the world is, on the whole, a green and pleasant place.

So, with the normal course of entry into graduate school, I came to find myself on a scientific expedition to the Great Barrier Reef. I was certain it would be the making of my future life. Here I shall get the chance to show the professionals that they need me on their staff. Certainly, though they never knew it, it was my gifts which guided them to where the sea snakes were. I was by far the best at counting starfish, and I could tell the spear-fishermen where the large coral trout were hiding, though that with a slight pang of guilt. I ate my brother the fish, figuring out, what the heck, I'm a carnivore like the rest, and who am I to place myself above my brethren in pain and suffering? It's a hard world down there, eat or be eaten, and a thousand different ways of doing it.

I'd have liked to tune in on my shipboard companions, but my gift had its limitations.

My first mistake was due to simple forgetfulness. We were on one of the smaller keys, though one with some vegetation, grasses mostly, and I was helping with the sampling.

'Need any help there, Frances?'

I looked up. It was Peter, the man from the marine park. He was definitely someone I wanted to impress with my qualities as a future employee. I knew I was looking good in my cut-down jeans and too-tight top, but I wanted to come across as more than that. I should have known better. It wasn't my body they were after. It was my mind which was to concern them.

Peter was thin and rubbery from a lifetime spent underwater, sampling the crown-of-thorns starfish and the rubbish from passing ships. 'Sea-floor litter is a terrible problem,' he'd say, sounding like a teacher doing yard duty, and I'd wonder if I really wanted a job with him doing the garbage run. But I warmed to him more as we hammered in the bright yellow stakes that marked our sampling spots. His secret love was turtles, he confided to me. I can only admire a man who loves turtles. The best part of his job, he said, was when he camped out on the lonely beaches where the turtles come to lay their eggs. Then, he'd hear them coming up the beach in the early hours of the morning. 'Chugga, chugga, chugga, like those machines that play space invaders.'

'I've been out with the turtle man. Stokesie, d'you know him? He's always there when they're laying. Before they know it, he's caught them, measured the distance between their eyes, clipped their flippers, and counted their eggs. He usually publishes six papers every laying season.'

'Mmm,' I said. 'Hey, do you know there's turtle eggs two feet down, under that yellow stake you're hammering in?'

'Hell, Frances, why didn't you tell me?' He turned white around the eyes, as only a turtle lover can. 'I could have damaged them.'

'No you haven't,' I said. I could hear the gentle murmur of life within.

Peter dug down to the eggs. 'It's true. How did you know that?'

I shrugged. Peter carefully replaced the stake. 'You're weird, Frances.'

'It's not me who's weird, it's everything else that's weird.' We looked around the coral island. So far, we had hammered in about twenty yellow stakes along a north-west transect. Karen was leaping about with a large white butterfly net, collecting insects. Greg was trundling a pedometer around the low-water mark. 'All right,' said Peter. 'We're normal, but he's weird.' Greg wore a yellow oilskin, green tracksuit trousers, legs unzipped to show wet socks and dirty sandshoes underneath. Greg gave us a wave. Then he stopped his measurements, frowned, and trundled his pedometer up the beach to us. Carefully, he rolled the pedometer over my leg.

'That's weird,' I said to Peter.

'Unacceptable margin of error,' muttered Greg, as he put his machine into reverse and made off down the beach to the shoreline. Scientific research is like that.

My second mistake happened soon after. That night, back on the ship, we sat at the same table, the professors and me, commensal, as they say in the world of protective hosts and protected guests. The barnacle on the carapace of the hawksbill turtle, or the anemone on the shell of the hermit crab both eat at the same table as their host carriers. The barnacle must wait for the turtle to take it to places where the plankton is plentiful. So the graduate student must rely on attaching herself to a professor who knows where the grant money flows freely.

Brodie was one of the best at attracting money. He could always be relied on to predict one natural disaster or another just before the grants money was handed out. 'Box jelly-fish terror,' the newspapers would announce, just as the jelly-fish season ended and the grants season began.

It was the joke session that did me in. 'Have you heard the one about Sara Pipelini?' asked Brodie, and we all said, 'No,' as one does. Up till then I had managed to laugh in all the right places, though I was troubled by stirrings deep beneath the ship. Something large was moving down there, and everything else was moving out of its way. I didn't notice when Brodie stopped talking, and I was far away when everyone else was laughing. These things add up, these moments of obtuseness, they count. The inability to see the point of a professorial joke may be interpreted as a lack of that empathic sensitivity to the group so necessary for the scientific teamwork of today.

The next day Jim came up to me. 'I'd like you to do me a favour.' Jim was a freelance ecologist noted for his zoological approach to love and life.

'After all, we have something in common,' said Jim, who liked his women uncomplicated and his booze straight.

'Well, don't we?'

'Do we?' I thought of his passion for motorbikes.

'We're both interested in proper reef management.'

I was relieved.

'Here's some notes I made last night. Look them over, and tell me what you think.'

He sat patiently by while I read. He had all the right buzz words, like ecological strategy, and the plant's investments in its genes, as if the natural economy mirrored the Aussie Bond. 'Techniques for survival in times of stringency', I read, but the theme was not today's graduate student in pursuit of a job, but the plant *Boerhaavia* striving to survive in the waterless sand and the wind of a coral key. As I read it, I realised he was making a fundamental mistake. It was the old problem of the observer and the observed, where the two may have very different perceptions of the same situation. How could I ever tell him that?

'That's as far as I've got at the moment,' Jim said, as I put the paper down.

'Nice,' I said. 'Neat.'

'Seriously, it's up your alley. Tell me what you think.'

Over on the reef, I could sense the crown-of-thorns starfish stirring. Peter was over there, counting them. They consider themselves an oppressed minority.

'Have you considered all the dynamics of the situation?' Disturbed by Peter's activities, a beche-de-mer extruded its digestive system through one end, and began rejecting its own insides.

'I think so.'

The complaints from the crown-of-thorns grew in volume. I held my hands to my head. I shut my eyes for concentration. I jerked back and forth as I thought of the plant *Boerhaavia*. 'Take the plant itself,' I said at last. 'It buries its thick, fleshy root two feet down into the coral rubble. But it's not the Darwinian notion of the struggle against a harsh environment that drives it on. No.'

'What do you mean?'

I should have stopped there, but the noise from the reef was dinning in my ears.

'What I'm saying is that it's a plant which is really into self-improvement. It burrows deep into whatever soil there is in order to keep in tune with the pulsing web of life. It likes to feel at one with the cosmos. Talk to it about ecological strategies and it simply won't listen. It knows perfectly well what it is about.'

Jim looked concerned. 'Frances, are you feeling all right?' He took his notes. Later, I saw him talking to Brodie. They looked my way once, then looked away again.

The sea snakes proved my ultimate undoing. Sad, that, because it was the best part of the trip. I could have come into my own as a sea snake catcher, but I let the boys do that. It's best not to poach the macho preserves. I helped where I could, in the water, snorkelling along, and acting as a sea snake spotter.

A sea snake spotter has a job, admittedly not the best job, but a sea snake spotter has a part to play in the grand scheme of things. It was pleasant in the water, floating over the edge of the reef, spotting a slight movement here, sensing a life coiled there. Naturally I was good at spotting, and the others soon learned to follow me. I would show them a tail pointing out of a coral outcrop, or a body neatly coiled under a ledge.

I despaired at what we did with the snakes, but then we did all that any non-empathic zoologist could do. We measured them, we weighed them, we determined their sex (two penises or none, nature in the case of the sea snakes overdetermining the issue). We cold branded a number on each snake, and then we put them back where we found them. The entire exercise would be repeated the next year, and the year after, and so the observations would go on, indefinitely, into the future.

The snakes knew more than could be told this way. I alone took pleasure in their awareness. I was filled with their golden fire.

'Here,' I shouted. 'Over here. Look, tracks of shining white.'

Jim came along, and down he went, and another snake swam into the catching net.

'There's another one! It's blue!' I yelled. When the snake proved the usual olive green, Jim swam up to me instead of the snake.

'You've been in the water too long. You're turning blue yourself. Go on back to the ship with this lot of snakes.'

'I'm all right. Look, it's just the light reflecting off that coral. Look how blue it is.'

Jim checked up on me. He looked under the water, and then at me. He looked as unconvinced as anyone can look in a face mask and a snorkel.

I stayed out a while longer, and then we got back into the dinghy with the snakes. We had to take them back to the ship after we'd collected twenty or so. I lifted the lid of the red plastic rubbish bin, and looked down at them.

No doubt about it, they were ropable. Chased, caught, and placed any old how on top of each other, they roared their indignation. Louder and louder, wilder and wilder, small pointed faces darting up the sides of the bin, and into the air above it. Each flash of their life ran electric through my mind, so that my gift, my albatross, fell. I called, 'Redemption!' And I put my arm down into their midst.

Jim watched, appalled.

They didn't bite my arm. But as I took my arm out, a green head brushed my cheek, and I felt the blood run down.

So here I am, sitting in the mess room, waiting. My companions are watching me carefully. They must watch for twenty hours, for only then will they know whether the fangs injected venom. They are watching me for signs, of drowsiness, of thirst. Only then will they know, to give the anti-venene. Meanwhile, they are murmuring. 'Your trouble is growing noticeable,' and 'It's overwork, it happens. People get over-anxious, they overdo it,' and 'It's been a considerable strain.'

I know now, that I could live ten thousand lives, and keep a record of their interactions, and it will never do me any good. Nature, by itself, is not enough. I am caught in a web whose significance I myself had spun. I am beginning to understand the harsh laws of life.

I am suddenly very tired.

Barry Westburg

IN THE MAIZE

The two of us were working our way across the field. Our step-grandmother had bully-coaxed us into doing it. Gunny sacks slung, dragging through the loam, catching now and again on roots, stubble. We picked the sweet corn in the long, arrowshot rows, stooping down, reaching up high. The isobars were crowding one another on the weather map but the sky I remember as colouring-book blue.

That was in Iowa. Corn was everywhere.

And because there was the full corn, Winter was ready to jab down from Canada's ice-fields and then we would be confined to tunnels of snow, more dead-straight rows. Cornstalks hissed, waved, muttered, and we were trying hard to bring full sacks back to Campbell.

Campbell was the farm lady who supplanted our real grandmother. Grandmother, an austere *memory* of a lady (handsome, white hair), lived in Denver with another old lady. She wrote to us three times a year: Easter, Christmas and on birthdays. What letters! The poetry of senile fancy, incomprehensible luxuriant caught-speech musings on her garden, pottings, mulchings, cuttings, creepers, the naughty cats' story cast in accents of fading birdsong, the gossamer never-recorded cadences of one old soul, bewildered in life's late garden heat.

But now we are concerned with Campbell — and shucking.

Picking it was not much fun, an overrated task, no amusement in it. But thereafter came the shucking . . .

It was nearing midcentury, when we were toiling up and down those corn rows. They were our family rows: opposite them the Olaffsen boys were doing their family rows too and beyond them you could see Michael Murphy (the sexfiend) all by himself as usual, but with a huge sack of corn bulging above him. The entire pre-pubertal male population of Strawberry Point was working those rows of Iowa corn. Quiet and businesslike, too, for behind each boy (a mile or so in the background) stood a threatening figure: a granny. A granny could wield a stick or a braided rope that was little less than a slavemaster's bullwhip when applied expertly to the burning body of a boy.

Ron was seven years old, a tow-head. I was nine but my hair was dark, curly and long. My mother and Campbell could not bear to see it cut. Dark curly hair was rare at Strawberry Point. Everybody was a tow-head, because almost everybody either came from Sweden or came from somebody who came from Sweden. The general principle and usage of the area was — to be Swedish. If you yelled out the name 'Oscar' about fifty boys and a hundred grown men might start running in your direction.

There are probably two or three people in the world who have not ever seen corn shucked properly. In Iowa where the entire lifestyle was based on the behaviour of corn, it would be as needless to describe cornshucking as it would to print eating directions on fried chicken (our other great staple). It was something you just knew how to do. Later on, for some of us, maybe, sex came naturally, too. But many others probably needed to have directions printed on their wives on their wedding night. For there must have been some fellows who never had a kid like Michael Murphy around to tell them how things were done.

The theory of shucking corn sets forth the uninterrupted gesture. One twist of the wrist and the ear must be laid bare. It was Michael Murphy who showed us how to apply this principle of physical economy to other things . . .

Once the corn was picked from each family row the boys would line up with their sacks at the tailgate of the shucking truck, a slat-sided flatbed stacked up with crates, each stencilled with a family name (a succession of alternating

-bergs, and -sens): Knudsen, Olaffsen, Svenberg, Pedersen, Flachsenberg, Murphy.

Murphy?

Michael Murphy, sexfiend, lived right next door to us. Ron was the first to surrender to Michael Murphy's tuition. In later life Ron confessed to me about some of these episodes but the length to which practical instruction was carried remains obscure, now clothed in nightweeds forever.

The paths of life are always dividing, forking: left or right, boy or girl, same or different. The lives of my brother and me diverged in corn-row and briar patch, again and again, until in later life it did not seem like we had ever been brothers at all. While Ron was learning about sex from a fiend, something different — call it an ideal — was being inserted into my brain. I was learning about love. The ideal of love came to me from comic books.

The comic book that most deranged me was called *Starry Eyes Comix,* which with admirable narrative gusto depicted the adventures of an impossibly beautiful girl-child. Her distinguishing feature was her starry bright-black eyes. The medium is the message: I fell in love with a cartoon.

Starry Eyes was cute the way Thumper and Bambi were cute. Big round eyes, long spiky lashes, a freckled button nose. And . . . chubby cheeks. And . . . a little ballerina's tutu! It was a *red, white and blue* tutu. Like Wonder Woman, whom I fell for later, she wore sexy-patriotic dress.

Lying on my back in the old three-storey frame house, I would stare at the ceiling, watching the chandeliers sway as if they had suddenly changed places with me and were sprouting up from the floor. Lying there with *Starry Eyes Comix*, throbbing with love, I would dream up hideous new adventures, new slobbering malodorous malefactors to menace her, creatures whom a cartoonist would never dare to draw, to test again and again her virtue, her grace under pressure, her inexhaustible supply of pure energy. She was fuelled by a terrible innocence and purity. And . . . God could she sparkle!

It was painful to love Starry Eyes, like loving any celebrity. She could not be coaxed down . . . from the imaginary firmament, so to speak. I'd cry over and over —

'Please Starry Eyes, come to see me, please please! Oh please, please, *please*!'

Please indeed.

My first wife, Donna, ex Mobile Alabama, would look as much like Starry Eyes as it was possible for any human being to do.

When the family rows of sweet corn were finally picked clean and the truck was loaded for the last time, the boys were carted off to the shucking. The women, girls and old men would be waiting at the shucking site. For in those days the grown young men, and the fathers, were off at the War, overseas somewhere.

Our father was a bomber pilot, then, away training new pilots in Texas, a job only slightly more dangerous than his previous one of flying missions over Germany.

So the shuckings were manless. It was a time for everybody else to get together without the bother of having men around. Clean old country gentlemen (honorary females), for once useful, would build the bonfires.

Ron and I jumped off the truck, followed by Michael Murphy. A sexfiend should slither: Michael Murphy *slithered* off the truck, last of us all.

'Fetch thet gunny sack over here, puddin',' Campbell said, knowing that I was the only one who would follow her say-so. Ron was always a little slow in following orders, like in everything else. In the natural economy of the family there has to be one smart and fast boy and a slow and retarded one to set him off. Ron spent the rest of his life trying to outlive that role (B.A., M.A., Ph.D., Harvard).

The clean old men set up the huge steel pots and filled them from the pump next to the farmhouse. The farmhouse was owned by real country people — the Torgissens — who rented out strips of 'acreage' for family planting. On the other side of the old stone house was more land for planting, too: the Strawberry Point graveyard. And beyond that, the church. The pots were for the cleanup, because after a few hours of shucking everybody is covered in corn-dust, like a mist.

It was not long before we loaded our first truck with bushels of shucked ears and the truck rumbled off down Merle Hay Road towards the communal silo. Merle Hay Road was named after the first Iowa boy careless enough to get himself killed in the war.

Meanwhile, in the farmhouse a mob of grannies was overseeing the fried chicken. Apricot pies were cooling on the back porch. Occasional forays by scent-crazed youths against these pies led to retaliatory search and destroy missions by the meanest and hardest of the granny-element.

The day wore on, and the truck came and went down Merle Hay Road for the last time. The pies cooled off, the chicken was brought out in tubs and exposed on the plank-and-trestle tables. The clean old men, after rescrubbing themselves in the pumpwater pots, were the first to eat. Somewhere, off in the larder, maybe, was the sacrosanct portion of dinner reserved for the grannies. They kept to themselves what was rumoured among us to be the choicest part: the giblets. Giblets! What are they? They were accomplishments of the chicken we boys never got to taste. I have met grown men who still do not know what a giblet tastes like, nor what general region of the chicken it comes from.

At some time during the evening the grannies would steal away, perhaps in small groups, perhaps one by one, to savour the giblets in the pantry. Nobody ever saw a granny actually eat. The younger boys were of the opinion that a granny *never* ate! The only boy who claimed ever to have seen a granny *in flagrante* with a giblet was Michael Murphy — but then out of his area of expertise he was considered an unreliable narrator.

After the clean old men were done, the girls were marched forward to the fried-chicken table. They ate daintily and only picked at their food. They wanted to keep their dresses clean for the dance later on. And since they didn't want to get sticky fingers from the chicken, they polished off the tomato salads — which by a lucky chance were an abomination to the boys. Our many cousins were among the foremost in this little procession. The prettiest of them were two sisters, Sharon and Liz. Between them (at a mere twelve and fourteen years of age) they had cornered the market on good looks.

The boys stood round the perimeter waiting for a shot at the fried chicken. They would have to move forward cautiously: there were a *lot* of grannies here, quite a brutal turnout of them in force, since most of the mothers had gone off to work at the John Deere plant on the swingshift — where they made bullets, grenades, and anti-personnel bombs.

By the time the boys licked the last of the chicken off their fingers, the sun was just about ready to drop down, as it does in the midwest. There was to be a full harvest moon that evening. And the harvest moon meant there would be dancing after dark. Without a moon dancing would be considered lewd and lascivious conduct. That's how the Iowa people thought.

'The Geezers', a five-piece string band of clean old men, began with the obligatory 'Turkey in the Corn'. My first partner was one of the smaller grannies, a wizened little number dark and hard as a horse-chestnut, not more than eighty or ninety years old. Ron was dancing with — among — the gigantic breasted Mrs Torgissen and later I saw him sent spinning about by cousin Liz, the elder of the sisters.

Then I was cast off by the granny and picked up by Sharon, who tried to waltz me around behind the shucking-mounds. There was danger of a kiss in this but, tired as I was from the picking, and the shucking, and weighed down with fried chicken, I still managed to manoeuvre Sharon out into the main ruckus of dancers, in company with Liz and her new partner, who happened to be Michael Murphy. They were doing some kind of wild jig to the waltz-time music. (Though The Geezers preferred jigs and reels above all music, they had been cautioned to concentrate on waltz-time, so as to preserve public order.)

After a great deal of fancy dancing and general showing off, Michael Murphy and Liz suddenly retired from the dancing-place, soaking with sweat, and I didn't see them for a while after that. Several hours later, somebody tripped over Liz, dishevelled, sleeping in a shucking-mound. Michael Murphy had slithered off somewhere, maybe to an urgent appointment.

— Behind the shucking-mound together?

— There's no great harm in that is there?

The harvest moon hung in the sky, like a firefly's answer to the sun or a detective's golden flashlight. I thought I could actually see its canals and hear its oceans, the waves sighing in the Sea of Tranquillity, the pounding of the surf on the Murphean Promontory . . .

— Whoa there. Send it past me one more time . . . *Murphean* Promontory?

— It's on the map of the moon, go and look it up, if you don't believe me!

I met Elizabeth Murphy, years later, in California, where most Iowans had migrated. It was right after her divorce from Michael. We had a few pina coladas together in the Gander Lounge of the Rusty Duck, in Laguna Beach. The break-up had been a messy affair. One day Michael had disappeared with their two boys and for several months Liz heard nothing about them. Finally, on the leading-edge of a nervous breakdown, Liz hired a private eye who eventually found the boys — in Australia. That's a story in itself, Liz said. Now she was planning to marry the detective, who got along terrifically with the boys. Sheldon needed a good woman in his life, after the troubles with Wanda.

As Liz got up to leave, I noticed that she still was a very attractive woman, that she had taken good care of her figure and was dressed expensively (a clinging dress in red, white and blue). But then every woman I knew those days dressed expensively and went heavy on the make-up.

Driving my Porsche back to the Laguna Plant of the Bernfax Corporation, I was turning management problems over and over in my mind, and somehow they got all tangled up with Liz's story about her kids (the eldest being named after me).

Passing the Laguna Beach Post Office, I suddenly had a thought. I pulled up at the self-service window and bought a picture postcard (a pale slice of moon shown hanging over Balboa Island). Taking my pencil to the picture side of the card, I quickly drew, superimposed upon the moonlit Pacific Ocean, a glistening row of cornstalks, petering out at infinity. On the flip side I addressed the card to Campbell Knudsen, Ogallalla Rest Home, Keokuk Iowa, and dropped it in the slot.

Rosa Safransky

POSTCARDS

When I was born, Europe became too crowded for my father, and he left. Two hotel rooms in Paris, with my uncle, mother and now me, was enough. Chips Rafferty decided him. Cattle crossing wild rivers, dancing, singing Aborigines. What could be less like Poland? My father had had enough of 'civilisation'. Enough of Auschwitz. A few postcards remain, written in Polish. My father's large hand addressed to my mother in Paris, 'Droga Elli'. My mother's neat microscopic scrawl to my father in Melbourne, 'Drogi Stan'.

A tailor, he imagined himself coming to the wildest, most uncivilised part of the globe. To a nation of Chips Raffertys in slouching digger hats with crooked friendly grins. But 'civilisation' proved harder to leave than he imagined. He spent his first nights in Melbourne at the George Hotel, confronted by an intimidating array of silverware and a waitress who called him 'Frenchie'. Feeling ill at ease, he could only point to the dishes he could not name. A few of the diners turned and stared, wondering if there was something wrong with him.

He mimed out these early dilemmas in front of Sunday afternoon guests, turning a chair into a plate, a lightfitting into a chandelier; changing our cramped weatherboard into the dining room of the George Hotel with an extravagant wave of his hand. As he talked, a Palm Court orchestra played softly from my uncle's bedroom. My mother laughed. The guests, wrapped in mothballs, sipped tea from their glasses and took extra slices of butter-cake.

My father and uncle made dresses for a living, manic-depressive dresses. We lived them, we ate them, we dreamed them. His mouth full of pins, he altered hemlines like a carpenter smashing nails into a piece of wood. Ulcers lay buried in his stomach like landmines. All it took to detonate them was a member of that brotherhood of thieves, his customers.

He came home one day in his loose-fitting suit which flapped as he walked. I heard the gate open and slam shut. I heard his shoes bite into the moss-covered earth. The kitchen door flew open and he appeared, coats and dresses over one arm, belts flapping wildly behind him. In a single heave, he threw the entire bundle onto the back of a nearby chair. His brown felt hat sat high on his forehead and when he took it off, a fine layer of sweat covered the inside. I saw again the strange pockmarks on his face, a daily reminder of the camps, and thought of the onion compresses my mother applied to his skin, and the medicine cabinet bursting with strange smells and remedies.

The season was bad. The vein on his forehead throbbed as he spoke. Wish me luck as you wave me goodbye my father sings. Nobody joins in, nobody laughs. My mother's face is dressed in a frown. Slowly the boot of the Morris is packed full of dresses. Everything is stapled inside cardboard boxes, including my father's song. When he says goodbye, a World War One poster, my mother, my sister and me, wave back at him.

The dresses, the Morris and my father plunge deep into the bush, across swollen rivers and mountains yet to be discovered. Soon postcards arrive in the mail. Civic fountains, statues of forgotten explorers, parks with benches in them and 'Welcome To The City Of Bathurst' in marigolds, petunias and dwarf chrysanthemums, stapled inside a flower-bed clock where time can only stand still.

Living at the centre of an industrial revolution, sewing machines tearing through fabric like rapid bursts of machine-gun fire, my father's nerves seemed often no stronger than the coloured threads he machined his coats and dresses with. The international hotel he shared with my two uncles, my mother and a soaring population of cats was a 'lunatic' asylum. My father and mother fought over everything. She irritated my father like the long underwear she bought him at bargain prices.

'Hairshirts. They itch!' he complained.

'You need to wash,' she said to him firmly.

My father hated washing. A cursory shake of hands under running water was enough. A bath was a Busby Berkeley production. He liked to wander around the house in his long woollen underwear, philosophising, before plunging in. But my mother was no Esther Williams. Her determined smile meant business.

She was a Renaissance woman. She had to be. Electrician, handywoman, scholar, cook, horticulturalist, military general. She was never short of things to do. No one understood my mother, least of all my father.

'If I don't do the cooking, who will do it . . . YOU? Who washes the dishes for me? Who gives me time to rest?'

My mother could not get through the thousand and one things she crowded her day with. She was Atlas supporting the globe on her back, carrying string bags bursting with fruit and vegetables from the market. Her shopping bags were so full that she tied them together with a handkerchief. There were always red marks on her hands when she put them down.

My mother was a fanatic. Her recycling had touches of genius in it. She could not even part with bits and pieces of old soap. They went into the drawers along with the mothballs. Nectarines and plums ripening on the windows often over-ripened and turned into green moulds. Stale bread became 'food for the birds'. Spiders were swept into a dust shovel and gently placed over the back fence; unless my father saw them first.

'What should we do, play with them?' he chided, wielding the end of a broomstick like an axe.

'Throw it out! Why do you keep it? Why do you hang on to it?'

The past always lived in the present. Throwing something out meant discarding another part of the past and my mother could never do that.

Old bread soaked in a tin saucepan was flung onto the roof each morning.

'Poor starving things,' she said of the gluttonous sparrows that gathered every morning, like needy friends paying her a social call. Our two cats lay in wait on a nearby roof pretending to doze, peering through eyes that were nothing more than slowly widening slits. Succulent juicy sparrows, ripe as bursting plums. I could see their fur ripple. I could almost hear them sigh. Sometimes they caught a bird and laid it at my mother's feet.

'Murderers! Murderers!' she screamed at them in Yiddish, sweeping them down the back steps in a fury. Slowly her thoughts returned to the dead bird.

'We'll have to bury the poor thing.'

My mother knew the secrets of the universe. I thought she was in touch with God, every morning out in the backyard. She prayed silently to Him, but I could see her lips move and sometimes I could make out a low hum of words. She kissed her blue prayer book which over the years showed traces of red lipstick around the edges. I watched her put lipstick to her mouth in the diamond-shaped mirror in the kitchen, smoothing it out carefully with a matchstick so the corners would not smudge. For my father it was all different.

'How could there be a God? What kind of God could let six million people perish in the gas ovens?'

No one had left Poland. The War had not finished. My mother was a photograph in the *Scourge of the Swastika* my father kept in the glove compartment of the car. My father still fought the gas chambers and concentration camps in his sleep.

Poland came to life every time my parents talked about it and ended when they stopped. As they talk, they paint a picture. A grandfather who ran a drozkie team in a small country town, a grandmother who hid in a cupboard every time there was lightning, another grandmother standing at her front door, calling all the names of her children, till she remembered the right one.

A collection of mysterious strangers inhabits my life, deposited in drawers, concealed in cardboard boxes along with postcards of fountains and the Eiffel Tower. Snapshots of streets and gardens and my mother, father and uncle, wearing double-breasted pinstripe suit smiles. I drew coloured rainbows on my sad-eyed Polish relatives. The Eiffel Tower is tinted blue, and pink clouds float in the sky. All of Europe is tinted blue and kept in a drawer. Melbourne felt like a turtle's back; my street was in the middle, Brunswick was somewhere near its edge, and if I went too far I might fall off.

My father screams out 'Elli!' to my mother who is preparing food in the kitchen.

'Come and dance!'

She shouts back 'I haven't got time!'

'She's always busy,' my father looks exasperated, sees me standing in the room, grabs me by the arm, and swings me over to the radiogram where a scratchy tango stops, starts and stops again. I look up at him and giggle through my missing front teeth.

'Elli, come and watch!' Again to no avail. So we start without her, me attempting to follow my father's steps in rough time to the music, jumping around till the floorboards shake, afraid of tripping over his feet.

My father had a weakness for opera singers. As he ironed or sewed, he whistled snatches from operettas. Every Sunday night we listened to 'A Life of Nellie Melba' on the radio, my father bent double over the sewing machine cursing a piece of thread which refuses to go through the needle. Melba is talking to her manager in Paris. They discuss her latest farewell performance. She is tired and cannot continue. Neither can my father as the stubborn thread unravels and breaks between his fingers. My mother arrives. She threads the needle in seconds. She is an expert. She never misses. Her shoulders hunch in concentration. She brings the needle and thread close to her face. She wets the thread between her lips and slides it through. Melba sings again. She must return to Australia. The music is sad. Violins play louder and I know she is going to die.

'How did she sing like that?'

'She had a strong voice and didn't give up,' he says offhandedly, machining linings into dresses till they are as stiff as boards.

Glenda Adams

THE VOYAGE OF THEIR LIFE

The rooster was crowing, at two in the afternoon, and the cicadas had started up again after their lunchtime quiet.

'It's a case of too much noise,' said Henry Watter, the father of Lark. 'Far too much noise.' He seized the hammer and rushed into the backyard. He thrust the rooster into a wooden crate and hammered it shut, the sun glinting on the hammerhead and on the lenses of his metal-rimmed glasses. The Bakers' dog next door started barking. The rooster continued crowing. From further off came the buzz of a lawnmower.

Lark looked through the old seventy-eights and the sheet music stacked near the pianola — Caruso singing '*Vesti La Giubba*,' a silly song called 'I Lift Up My Finger and I Say Tweet, Tweet'. She had already saved a hundred pounds, almost enough for a one-way passage to somewhere, Singapore or Ceylon perhaps, or even Kansas, and she had arranged for an interview with Qantas to be an air hostess, after her exams. That was one way to get away.

Lark's father rushed into the house, then returned to the backyard with several army blankets and an old Belgian flag, which he draped over the crate, layer on layer, creating night for the confused bird.

'Sits there like a stunned mullet,' said Henry Watter.

'Do you think that's wise, Henry?' asked Lark's mother from under her pink cloth sun hat. Her hands, in white gloves, were pegging clothes on the line with such alacrity that she could have been playing a scherzo on the pianola. The gloves protected her hands from the sun. The sun hat, in addition to performing its intended function, protected her head from the kookaburras and magpies, which liked to swoop down to take strands of hair for their nests.

'Like bombers,' said Henry Watter. 'It's a case of World War Two in our own backyard. This country's a joke. One big joke.'

The crowing continued, muted, while he lobbed stones at the yelping dog next door. Every now and then he threw a stone into the trees to silence the cicadas. And he stood, waiting for the next noise, in his singlet and khaki shorts, which were held up by a piece of rope tied around his waist in a reef knot. His feet, in black nylon ankle socks and lace-up shoes, looked as if they had been planted and had sprouted those white legs now trembling with rage.

The lorikeets, fifty or sixty of them, started lining up on the veranda rail, jostling and squawking, peering in the window, arranged in a multi-coloured *tableau vivant*, waiting for the daily bread that Lark's mother put out for them. Taking care of Australia's natural heritage, she called it.

Lark's father took a mop and waved it at the birds on the veranda rail. 'Heritage be damned,' he said. 'In this flaming country it's a case of too much nature. Far too much nature.'

'Henry, please, no language,' whispered Lark's mother.

'Where's that cat when it's needed?' Henry Watter muttered. He swung at the birds. 'William the First,' he said and swung again. 'William the Second,' and he swung again. 'Henry the First, Stephen.'

'Watch my windows,' called Lark's mother from under her hat. 'They'll cost the earth to replace.'

'Henry the Second, Richard Lionheart, John.' Lark's father threw the mop down beside the back steps and stamped inside.

'Mind my parsley and my mint,' said Lark's mother.

'William and Mary,' said Lark's father. 'Far, far too much nature.'

Lark had always planned to run away. When she was four, she had packed her little cardboard sewing case with her supplies for the journey — a swimsuit, an umbrella, her money box, and a little bottle of water — and kept it under the bed, next to the large black umbrella that could also be used as a walking stick. She wanted to wander around and around the world, until she found some kind of island to settle on.

'I'm going now,' she often said, taking the suitcase and umbrella, standing at the front door.

'She's going now,' they said, if they said anything at all.

And sometimes she went along the cliff road, above the Pacific Ocean, past the school, as far as the corner.

In that house in Park Avenue on the cliff in Sydney, Henry Watter sat memorising *Bartlett's Familiar Quotations*.

Lark was dumping her books in a canvas bag.

'Test me,' Lark's father said.

The lorikeets were at the window, nudging the glass, tapping it with their beaks, chattering.

'I was just going down to the beach to study,' said Lark.

'Test me first,' said her father. He, too, had been preparing to run away for years.

Lark sighed. 'Kings of England? Shakespeare? Definitions?'

Henry Watter pointed at the street map of London pinned across the bookshelves.

'Streets of London, then,' said Lark.

The muffled cries of the rooster still reached them.

'God love a duck,' said Henry Watter. And then, 'God stone the crows.'

The Bakers' dog was still yelping.

'How do you get from Regent's Park Zoo to,' Lark searched for somewhere for him to go, 'to the Tower of London?'

When Lark was young, Henry Watter had taken her to the zoo, the Sydney Zoo, and at the end of the day had said, 'Let us catch the ferry now and go home.' Lark thought he had said he was going to catch a *fairy*, and she was in some state of excitement as they walked down the path to the harbour. At the wharf, when he asked 'Is this the ferry to the

Quay?' the boat hand nodded and they boarded. 'Where's the fairy?' Lark asked, and her father said, 'You're on it'. It felt like a cruel joke. Lark ran onto the wharf and refused to get back on the ferry. Her father had to get off, too, and the ferry left without them. That particular ferry caught fire in the middle of the harbour and the passengers had to take to the lifeboats. Several of them drowned. They all said it was Lark's sense of impending doom that had saved them.

Henry Watter settled in his chair, turning his back on the map. He pushed his glasses on top of his head. His voice became soft and slow. 'Turn left on Marylebone Road, then south on Tottenham Court Road, which turns into Charing Cross Road, to Trafalgar Square. Then turn left on The Strand. Keep going.' And he kept going, until he ended up at the Tower. 'Of course,' he added, 'you could go out the northern end of the park, near Primrose Hill, and walk along the footpath beside the canal to Camden Town, then take the tube.' He took care to explode the 't' in tube. 'You see, Larkie, I'll get along there, when I go. I can say tube like an aristocrat, instead of chube like a pleb.'

'I'm going to the beach now,' said Lark. 'I have to study my French.'

'Just one more, Larkie, please,' pleaded Henry Watter.

'But I'll really need my French, when I go,' said Lark.

'And I'll need to know my England.'

Lark sighed. 'Name three of Shakespeare's clowns,' she said, 'not including poor Yorick.'

The lorikeets were calling out. The tableau had broken formation and the birds were falling over one another in anticipation.

Henry Watter placed *Bartlett's Familiar Quotations* in Lark's hands, 'Test me, Larkie.'

She let the book fall open. '"There is a tide in the affairs of men, which, taken at the flood, leads on to fortune."'

Henry Watter sat up straight. ' "Omitted, all the voyage of their life is bound in shallows and in miseries." W. Shakespeare, J. Caesar. Act four, scene three.'

Mrs Watter was putting out the bread soaked in milk and

honey. The beaks of the lorikeets hit the tin pans like gravel falling on a tin roof.

'Get the cat,' cried Henry Watter. 'Set it on those birds.' He fell back into his chair. He shook his head for a while, then picked up the dictionary and continued to memorise it. 'Martello tower,' he said. 'A circular, masonry fort.'

'But you'll note,' said Lark's mother, 'that sometimes he holds the book upside down. I do believe he thinks he is a writer or something. He keeps scribbling things in an exercise book. I find it under the mattress when I turn the bed.'

With her books under her arm and the beach umbrella over her shoulder, Lark walked along Park Avenue to the path that led to the beach. She hoped to find Solomon White there. They had started doing things together, going out. The night before, they had seen *Cat on a Hot Tin Roof* and Solomon had asked Lark if she could put on her nylons the way Elizabeth Taylor had in the movie, a kind of peeling-on motion. Lark had said she thought she could. And they were to go to the Recovery Ball together, after Lark's exams. Solomon had graduated and no longer had final exams, only his research, and he was waiting to hear from the dozens of universities abroad, where he had applied to do his doctoral research.

Solomon's younger brother, Marshall, was in the schoolyard, mowing the lawn, earning his pocket money. That was a good sign. It seemed to mean that the Whites were around, not off at their country house or at a luncheon in the eastern suburbs.

The three White boys were named after islands in the South Pacific — Gilbert, Solomon and Marshall.

'Better than Guam,' Solomon said, 'Or Nauru.'

'I wish I were named after an island,' cried Lark, 'or that an island were named after me.'

'You'd have to own one,' said Solomon, who had already travelled a lot. 'Then you could name it what you wanted.'

The Whites were the most exotic family in Park Avenue.

Mr and Mrs White had even taken their three sons to England for a year, for the culture, when they were all very young. Solomon's great-grandfather, Charles White, and his great-grandmother were said to have Christianised the entire South Pacific. It had been ascertained that Charles White had drunk with Robert Louis Stevenson. And he would have conducted the service in 1914 when the ashes of the storyteller's wife were brought to Samoa, if a storm had not prevented his boat leaving the island where he was proselytising at the time.

Lark pushed hard on the rusty metal catch of the old canvas umbrella. Another year and she should have enough money to go away. She lay on the sand and started with *L'étranger*, trusting that sentences like, 'I was almost blinded by the blaze of light', 'the sand was hot as fire', and 'now and then a longer wave wet our canvas shoes' would be useful during her future adventures, away. Two flies buzzed around her, alighting on her lips and nostrils, and, as she read, she had to keep brushing her hand against her face.

Solomon White threw his car keys on the pages of Lark's book. She had not sensed his walking towards her across the sand. '*La campagne bourdonnait du chant des insectes*,' she said to Solomon. 'The countryside was throbbing with the hum of insects. I'll be needing that, when I go away.'

Solomon was shaking his head to get rid of the two flies, which had transferred their attention to him. He sat on the sand beside her and rubbed suntan oil on her back.

'Can you justify the following being regarded as a short story?' Lark asked, looking out to sea. 'What does the author achieve within the severe limits he has set himself? That's the kind of question I'm going to have to answer.' She continued quoting. '" 'To die like Joan of Arc,' said Terbaud, from the top of a pyre built with his furniture. The Saint-Owen fire-brigade hindered him."'

Solomon laughed. 'That's not a story.'

'Why not? You have plot, character, a protagonist who wants something urgently, in this case, a death like Joan of Arc's, an antagonist, in this case the fire-brigade, you have a sense of time and place,' said Lark. 'That's all a story needs. Three lines. Less.'

And then Mrs Baker came huffing past, since it was Saturday and not a sign of turpitude to be on the beach, and stopped to shout that it was a hot day, like a furnace. Solomon continued to rub the oil on Lark's back, Lark agreed that it was a hot day, and Mrs Baker passed on to pitch her umbrella a little further along the sand next to a friend, and her chattering began again. 'Like a parakeet in a cage,' Lark said.

Lark's mother remarked that Mrs Baker had seen Lark on the beach with a young man.

'I was with Solomon White,' said Lark.

Lark's mother asked what he had been doing.

Lark frowned and thought. 'Possibly he was helping me put up the umbrella.'

'Mrs Baker said that Solomon White was rubbing oil on your body.'

'That's right,' said Lark. 'That's what he was doing.'

'Then why didn't you say so?'

From his chair Henry Watter called, 'Get thee to a nunnery.'

And Lark thought it would not be long now before she left.

'I'm leaving,' Solomon White had told Lark as he smoothed the oil over her back and arms. 'I have the fellowship. Champaign-Urbana. I am going forever.'

Lark had hunched over her book. She wished that Solomon would fail at something. '*Rester ici ou partir, cela revenait au même,*' she'd said, surly. 'To stay here or to leave, it comes to the same thing.'

'Sour grapes,' said Solomon. 'You'll be going soon, too. Everyone does.'

They went down to the water's edge and walked along the bright sand to the sandstone rock platform at the base of the weathered cliff. The sun glinted on the mica and quartzite fragments in the stone. The seagulls picked at the bits and pieces of oysters and periwinkles. The sea was calm. The waves welled up, rose, like a loaf of bread, and spilled gently across the rock shelf, wetting their feet. They lay down together on the rocks. The water, tepid from its journey across the warm rock shelf, slid under their backs. Lark's head rested on Solomon's shoulder.

'You're giving me a golden shoulder,' he said, and kissed her. 'Perhaps you'll end up with me in Champaign-Urbana. Who knows?'

'End up?' said Lark. 'We would just be beginning.' She sat up and watched the seagulls. 'I want to go to Paris. You'd like living in Paris, too,' she quoted. 'And of course we could travel about France for some months in the year.'

'Paris?' said Solomon, puzzled, sitting up. 'I have to go to America. Sometimes I have absolutely no idea what you're talking about.'

'Camus,' said Lark.

Very far out a ship was gliding past, a freighter heading north, for Newcastle or Gladstone, and then possibly further, across the Pacific to America.

'Could I come with you now?' Lark had asked into Solomon's shoulder.

'I'll write,' Solomon had said. 'I'll tell you what it's like, away. We'll see what happens. I'll miss you, you know.'

'Can you justify the following being regarded as a short story? "Silot, a valet, established an attractive woman in the home of his absent master at Neuilly, then disappeared carrying away everything but her."'

'You didn't go around the rocks, did you?' asked Lark's mother.

'I don't remember,' said Lark.

'Mrs Baker said you went around the rocks with him,' said Lark's mother. 'You know what happens around the rocks. It's not nice for one thing, and for another the waves can be dangerous. They can kill.'

'He's leaving,' Lark said. 'You don't have to worry about him and me any more. He's off, lucky devil.'

'Please, Lark, no language,' said Mrs Watter.

Lark walked slowly along the cliff-top road from the house to the little school with the iron fence. Solomon White had flown off to America.

'We'll have to fly,' Mrs Watter had said once, when Lark was very young and they were running late for the bus into town. Mrs Watter had seized Lark's hand and run down the front path, hauling Lark along, who expected that at any moment they were to rise into the air and fly to the bus.

Lark stopped at the school gates, leaning her forehead against the bars, her eyes closed. The cicadas were shouting, like a male chorus, causing the air to throb, the sound waves almost palpable. She heard again those mouth organs, the recorders, triangles, tambourines, little drums and the sound of spoons beating against saucepans and saw those children, some fifty of them, parading in a cicle around the school lawn, looking neither happy nor sad. The older ones, Solomon White among them, were playing the musical instruments, the younger were banging the spoons and saucepans. Lark was crying because she had only two spoons to beat together. The headmistress stood on the school veranda and announced several times, wringing her hands, 'We have won the war in Europe, children. God was on our side. The Germans have been brought to their knees. We have cut them down.'

A girl who was a celebrity in the school because she had been in England when the war broke out was allowed to plant a tree in a special ceremony.

'VE Day will be our May Day forever more,' said the headmistress. 'And now there remains only the Pacific to be won.'

In the cloakroom Lark stole the woollen beret of the girl who had planted the tree. She crammed her own panama hat on her head, trying to tuck the beret under it, out of sight. When the girl cried that she could not find her beret, the teacher seized Lark's panama and reclaimed the beret. Her face leant down into Lark's.

'Two hats?' the teacher said, sarcastic, dangling both in Lark's face, humiliating her in front of all the children. 'Get your own beret, if you want one.'

But with wartime rationing, only the rich had woollen berets.

'What is May Day?' Lark asked her father.

'Mayda?' He sat up, his book face down on his knees, delighted with the question. 'Mayda is a legendary island south-west of Ireland, and west of Brittany.'

'May Day?'

'Oh, you mean Mayday! That's an international distress call. Do you want me to teach it to you?'

'No,' said Lark.

Then she remembered leaning against the mulberry tree and watching her mother chop the head off a chicken. The body ran around the yard. The Pacific war was over and they were celebrating with a chicken dinner. The Bakers took down the flags of the Allies, which they had flown every day of the war. They offered the Belgian flag to Lark, the little girl next door. Lark was surprised that the black, yellow and red cloth was woollen and extremely rough to the touch. She wrapped the flag around her, like a cloak. She put on her father's gas mask and crept to the fence and peered over at the Bakers' boy. He ran to his mother, screaming that there was a monster on the back fence, and Mrs Baker told him that the Watters were a strange lot.

'Ask me the stops on the air route from Sydney to London,' Henry Watter said to little Lark. 'It won't be long now before I go.' Then he continued, without waiting for her to form the question, 'Sydney, Brisbane, Gladstone, Townsville, Karumba, Groot Island, Darwin, Kupang, Bima, Surabaja, Batavia, Klabat Bay, Singapore, Penang, Bangkok, Rangoon, Akyab, Calcutta, Allahabad, Gwalior, Karachi, Gwador, Dubai, Bahrein, Basra, Tiberias, Athens, Brindisi, Rome, Marseilles, Macon, Southampton, London.'

Lark lifted her head from the fence rail. The cicadas, accompanied by lawnmowers, were still at it.

To her Qantas interview Lark wore a floral blouse

buttoned to the neck and a dark-green linen skirt with four buttons at the back, forming the four points of a square, like the buttons on a man's double-breasted jacket. She thought she looked rather like an air hostess already. 'With those buttons, I hope you don't have to sit down,' Lark's father said. In her coat pocket she carried Solomon White's first letter.

The secretary told her to take off her coat before she went in to the personnel officer. 'He has to check your deportment,' she said. So Lark abandoned her coat and entered the huge office, where a man in a brown suit sat behind a desk at the far end and watched her deportment as she walked to him.

'Why,' he asked, 'do you want to be a Qantas air hostess?' He tapped a pencil against his finger, as if he had asked a riddle about the meaning of life.

Lark hesitated. She thought of saying she had always admired Qantas and had wanted to serve that particular company ever since she was little.

'I want to leave Australia,' she said. 'I want to go away.'

She had to walk out again, across that vast floor, with that personnel officer watching those four buttons and judging.

'The bermuda season has arrived here and both men and women are gaily decked in the new season's colours and subtle variations of cut and style,' Solomon White wrote. 'And here is a piece of oneupmanship you might like to have at your fingertips. The word is "rain check". I called a girl to ask her for a date — you have to go out on dates in America, it's the done thing, it doesn't mean anything — and she said she was very sorry, she couldn't make it but would I give her a rain check please. I said, yes of course, but being a cautious soul I inquired what it was I had just given her.' Solomon White seemed to be in the most exciting place in the northern hemisphere. And while he had not mentioned again that Lark might join him, he had said that he remembered her head resting against his shoulder and that he missed her.

'I feel now that it is time for me to attend to other matters,' Solomon had ended his letter. 'So if you will excuse me I will just pour myself another bourbon and squirt from the cocktail bar and make a graceful exit through the kitchen, where the pretzels and beer nuts are kept.'

Lark was informed that she was not the right material for an air hostess.

She searched through the Saturday *Herald* for jobs abroad, governesses wanted, anywhere, fares paid.

'We had an air raid today according to the radio,' Solomon had written. 'But since I didn't see any aeroplanes or bombs I can only assume that it was a hoax, a failure on somebody's part, or perhaps a civil-defence effort. I was in Washington, D.C., with a friend during our semester break and viewed the Constitution, the Bill of Rights, and the Declaration of Independence in their bombproof, shock-proof, fireproof, helium-filled vault. The traditions of America are very obvious to one and all and, quite seriously, I came away very impressed. I can now think of America as something more than a plastic hot dog, a huge imperialist financial machine and the home of the Midwest.'

And then he had added, 'Summer in Champaign-Urbana is a time for socialising in a capitalistic sort of way, and I am drastically short of money. Yesterday a young lady and I went out stealing peaches and tomatoes from the university orchard. It doesn't mean what you think. In America it's just a social necessity to date.'

In the library among the many books written by various Charles Whites, Lark found one by a Charles White who was the first man to ride a single horse across the North American continent, from Catalina Island in California to Coney Island in New York. She copied this information out and sent it to Solomon White, in the middle of the North American continent. 'Why don't we do something inventive like your ancestor?' she wrote. 'We could write a book about it. Together.'

Solomon White wrote and told Lark that he was facing a long, hot, lonely summer and could no longer do without the steady companionship of a female. He had succeeded in meeting a tall, fairly attractive, fairly blonde American. They had been to New York together. 'It's the most exciting place I've been to,' he wrote. 'You should see the real Park Avenue.' And some weeks later Solomon White's mother conveyed to Lark the good news that Solomon was getting married to a fairly tall, really beautiful American blonde. And Solomon's letters to Lark stopped altogether.

Lark dreamed she was waiting for a New York subway to whisk her off to an unknown destination. When the train hurtled into the station, it bore the sign, 'Beware the deadly gases of Atmium and Thomium.' It was definitely her train. She had to board it, although she had no gas mask.

At dinner Lark said, 'I'm going now.'

'This bird is tough,' said Henry Watter. He looked up. 'She's finally going?'

'To Paris,' said Lark. 'Or New York.'

'What do you want to go there for?' Henry Watter asked. 'England's the only place.' He chewed at his food, looking at each piece on his fork before he put it in his mouth. 'Tough old bird. Just like your mother.'

'It's that Solomon, isn't it?' said Mrs Watter.

Lark shook her head. 'I always meant to go.'

'Well, at least we finally got rid of that rooster,' said Henry Watter, chewing.

'And you'll get married of course.'

Lark shrugged.

'Just like a war bride,' said Lark's mother. 'I remember them after the war, so excited to be going away. I wanted to go, too.'

'No more crowing in the middle of the flaming day,' said Henry Watter. He looked at Lark. 'I chopped its damned head off, you know. We're eating it.'

'Please, Henry, language,' said Lark's mother.

'Throw me the gravy,' said Henry Watter.

'Please, Henry, pass,' said Mrs Watter, handing him the gravy boat. She stared out the window. 'I used to go down to Pyrmont to see the boats off and throw streamers to all those soldiers and their war brides, sailing off across the Pacific at the end of the war. We'd hold onto the streamers as if we might be taken along, too.'

Henry Watter held the gravy in the air, making it sail along, up and down, like a toy boat on the sea. 'Take the current when it serves,' he said.

'Henry, please, manners.'

'J. Caesar. A self-made man. Like N. Bonaparte. Self-made men,' said Henry Watter. He stood up. 'And so to bed.'

Lark's mother stayed a moment longer at the table before clearing away the dishes. 'We even thought the men going off to war were lucky to be travelling,' she said softly. 'When I was a little girl, I was taken down to the Quay to wave them off to Gallipoli, as if they were going on a holiday. It was very jolly. And only much later did we learn what Gallipoli really was, that Churchill and our own government had betrayed us.'

Lark's earliest memory was a picture in the Sydney newspaper. An Australian soldier, a prisoner in the Changi camp in Singapore, was about to be beheaded by a Japanese holding a sword. He was kneeling, his arms tied behind his back, his head bowed. To spare his family at home, the soldier's face had been blacked out.

'A good thing we got the bomb first,' shouted Henry Watter from the bathroom.

'So much noise.' Lark's mother shook her head. 'Sometimes,' she whispered. 'I have absolutely no idea what he's talking about.'

Lark helped with the dishes, then went to her room to pack her things for the voyage.

Frank Moorhouse

CULTURAL DELEGATE

As a cultural delegate, Blase tried always to read the protocol guides to the sensitivities and customs of other nationalities. Although he knew in his heart that he was a bad cultural delegate he did, at least, worry about protocol.

He knew, for instance, that the Chinese were punctual and took speech-making and banqueting seriously. This pleased Blase, himself no mean banqueter back home and also known as something of a speech-maker. He knew that the Chinese did not dress formally and Blase decided to confine himself to an elegantly tailored Mao jacket and cap from Bucks of Melbourne.

He knew that, when the Chinese clap you, you are expected to clap them in return. With the Chinese you avoided excessive physical contact and boisterous behaviour. He knew about giving gifts to institutions and not to individuals and that expensive gifts such as automobiles and computers were embarrassing to the Chinese (advice which came as a relief to Blase, who liked to travel 'heavy', but not that heavy).

He knew not to tip and he knew not to give the Chinese nicknames. He knew not to display affection publicly and not to show anger either to other members of the delegation or towards the Chinese. There were to be no punch-ups. He knew there was also to be no public drunkenness and that the Chinese were moralistic about sex. And guests leave banquets ten minutes after the hot towels.

So although he was no good at inspecting things, could not remain attentive and questioning for long periods and had no interest in magnificent scenery, Blase at least knew his protocol.

Consequently, Blase went to his first banquet in his elegant Mao jacket and cap and with a pocketful of cheap kangaroo pins and was devastated when the Chinese turned up in dinner suits. They were also a bit drunk, slapped everyone on the back, threw food at each other, kissed him on the mouth, grabbed his genitals at every occasion and asked not too subtly for gifts, including automobiles and motorbikes.

He was offered sex, and the party did not stop ten minutes after the hot towels, but went on into the early hours. Later they all crept into an army barracks and stole a People's Liberation Army flag.

Next day in the bar of the Jing Jiang Club, recovering from his hangover, Blase, in his food-stained Mao jacket and cap, asked his Guide what had gone wrong. Blase had a profound sense of cultural confusion. The Guide was still drunk and they had shaken off the rest of the delegation, who were wandering lost in the alleys of Shanghai.

At first the Guide wouldn't explain, but after being given a Chinese burn he revealed that the Chinese, too, had been briefed on protocol for handling Australians. The Guide gave Blase a translation.

Australians are easy-going about time and punctuality and consider it over-conscientious to be on time. To be late is to protest against despotic employers.

Australian men like to dress up in dinner suits as a way of aping their former aristocratic rulers. Australians enjoy physical contact and there are hotels in Australian cities where men go to kiss other men and hold hands; likewise women. This is becoming the custom.

Australians like to tip and give gifts as a way of showing their generosity, as a way of rewarding good service and as a way of aiding poor nations.

Australians like to break time-honoured rules and customs as a way of showing their independence from the chains of the past — for example, climbing to the top of a sacred monument and placing a beer can there, stealing a Chinese flag from an army barracks, diving into ponds and trying to catch century-old goldfish. This is called Larri-kin-ism.

Australians are accustomed to indulging their sexual appetites at every available opportunity, especially while travelling in other countries, which is considered to be a 'holiday from marriage'. Singsong girls should be found for Australian males and Chinese studs for Australian women.

Australians like to make jokes at each other which is called 'taking the mick-ie'. Australian men sometimes grab each other's genitals as a gesture of comradeship known as Goo-sing.

Australian women like to take off their tops at every opportunity for sunbathing and prefer not to wear bras. But Chinese men should practise the Three Nos laid down by the last People's Congress — 'No staring, No touching and No funny business'.

Australian language is rich in animal imagery and so they say horsing around, goo-sing, snake in the pocket, no bull-defecation and they like to go on what they call pussy hunts. Australians become angry if they think that a person is bull-defecating.

Australians are artistic people who sometimes build elaborate sculptures from beer bottles or beer cans while drinking. They will sometimes take the Guide's hat and throw it around, one to the other, but this must be seen as a need to release excess energy from a high protein diet and short working week.

Australian men are also forever fly-checking. This is not a sexual gesture but an old horse-riding custom to reassure themselves that no injury has befallen that part.

Australian men may be observed smelling bicycle seats because, as a nation of horsemen (see film, *The Man from Snowy River*), the smell of the bicycle seat reminds them of the saddle of the horse back home which they miss.

Souveniring: Australians come from a penal colony and,

as a remembrance of their ancestors, still like to practise 'symbolic theft' as a gesture against the rich. They will often take things they do not need from a public place; for example, you may see them trying to take a park bench home. Pay no heed.

When doing business with Australians, Chinese should beware of the saying, 'I'll toss you double or nothing'.

Beware of such Australian expressions as 'Let's talk about it over lunch' (they will try to get you drunk), 'Let's leave the details to the accountants', 'Of course there is a little something in it for you', 'We don't want the taxman getting his hungry little hands on any of it', 'I don't think there's any need to put that in writing', 'One for you, one for me and one for the family trust', 'I have a little off-shore company that handles those problems', 'Something's come a little unstuck but it's all under control — my MD does what I tell him', 'We're in a grey area but that's my reading of the investment guidelines — let's give it a punt', and 'We'll handle the documentation at our end if you like'.

Never do business with an Australian who says 'no worries' a lot.

That the Chinese knew so much about the Australian soul plunged Blase into deep gloom and he and the Guide stayed in the Jing Jiang Club for two days playing billiards with the New Zealand Female Steeple-Jumping Delegation.

From the Leader of the Delegation

The members of the delegation feel that Francois Blase should not be a cultural delegate in future. Or, in fact, represent his country in any capacity.

While abroad, he mopes in his room too much. He is apathetic about scenery. He does not seem to know what to say about scenery. He sometimes refuses to look at it. He says it makes him 'ineffably sad'.

He does not know the words of 'Waltzing Matilda'. He is uncertain about how much iron ore Australia produced last year. He often will not come out of his room despite efforts by the Leader of the Delegation and the Guide. He pretends to be ill.

He refused to go into an ancient Buddhist temple built without the use of nails 'because,' he said, 'if a Buddhist temple is going to fall, it will be me it falls on.' Sometimes he refuses to leave the car saying that he 'will watch from the window'. While the rest of the delegation goes inspecting, he drinks beer with the driver and listens to the car radio.

When our hosts ask the delegation what it is they would like to see, Blase says 'anything with blood on it'. He asks to be taken to war museums and museums of the people's uprising, knowing full well that cultural delegations are about peace and friendship and not about how many rounds a minute the AK-47 fires.

He spends days at a time in the Jing Jiang Club and such places with the New Zealand Female Steeple-Jumping Delegation. He does Chinese breathing exercises to the embarrassment of his hosts. He smuggles things in and out of countries using his Official Passport. Some days he asks no questions. He hums the song 'Moon River' to annoy the rest of the delegation. He seems morbidly interested in starvation and infant mortality.

He embarrasses the Guide by asking all the time about what he calls 'jig jig'. He makes long speeches at the banquets out of turn and alludes to 'dark things of the soul'. At the performance of *The Official and His Five Daughters* by the all-female cast of the Hangzhou Opera Company, he went backstage and pursued the juvenile lead and persisted in inviting her back to the hotel for 'supper'.

In Shanghai he invited the Jolly Cooks and the Jumps From the Spring Board Performers back to the hotel after the acrobatics and we've heard that the Jolly Cooks did not appear the following night (the first performance they've missed since the troupe was formed twelve years ago). They kept the whole hotel awake singing 'Moon River'.

On the train trip to Guiling he took out a pack of cards and went 'looking for some action'. We did not see him for sixteen hours and we heard that he taught poker to the attendants and won from them the equivalent of their year's wages. When we remonstrated with him about this he said: 'That's what I call cultural exchange.'

His business card is supposed to be 'amusing' but leaves much to be desired in the area of good taste. Loosely translated, it says something like 'Master of Jig Jig'.

Enclosed is a recording of a 'cultural exchange' Blase had with a Mr Cao in Beijing which we submit as supporting evidence:

'Tell me, Mr Cao, in our country we have a saying that the hunter must know the animal he stalks. Do you think that is the purpose of cultural exchange? Is that what our leaders have in mind?'

The Guide translates. Mr Cao laughs and then replies in Chinese.

Guide: Mr Cao says yes, we too hunt in the outer provinces. The peasants hunt for hare.

Blase: I do some hunting myself. Do you need a licence to own a gun in China?

Mr Cao laughs and replies.

Guide: Mr Cao says that in our country we have a saying: 'The dogs bark, the caravan moves on.' Do you have such a saying?

Blase: We say that the dog that does not bark may still bite. I see very few dogs in your country. I believe they are eaten.

The Guide translates. Mr Cao laughs and replies.

Guide: Mr Cao says that in your country he believes dogs are raced for amusement.

Blase: Does Mr Cao eat dogs?

The Guide translates. Mr Cao laughs and replies.

Guide: Mr Cao says it is too early to eat, but if you are hungry he will buy an ice on the stick. Do you have ice on the stick in your country?

Blase: We have 200 varieties of ice on the stick, including one called Dracula's Blood.

The Guide translates. Mr Cao laughs and replies.

Guide: Mr Cao says we have a folk tale called the Ice Fairy in which a young man falls in love with a beautiful woman, not knowing that she is made of ice. In the spring ... But it is a long story and a sad story. We do not have time.

Blase: We have women made of ice in our country.

The Guide translates. Mr Cao laughs and replies.

Guide: Mr Cao is surprised you have ice in your country. We believe it to be desert.

Blase: We have mountains on the coast. But there is much desert and it could not support a large population — if a large population suddenly were to come there. What calibre shot gun does Mr Cao have?

The Guide translates. Mr Cao laughs and replies.

Guide: Mr Cao says he owns a 12-gauge Winchester over and under. He says why don't we stop this faeces about folk tales and iron ore production and grab a couple of dozen cold cans and go shoot everything that moves in the forest.

Blase: Tell Mr Cao that suits me fine.

Mr Blase and Mr Cao then left the party and refused to rejoin it for the completion of the day's itinerary. They allegedly shot beer cans in the Forest of International Harmony.

We recommend that Francois Blase not represent Australia on any further delegations. If the Department receives letters approving of Mr Blase from Mr Cao, the Jolly Cooks, the Jumps From the Spring Board Performers or the juvenile lead of the Hangzhou Opera, we suggest they be evaluated in the light of this report.

(signed) Leader of the Delegation

Don Watson

GD SHIP COUNTRY

It was Abel Tasman, once more in search of ginger, who first exclaimed on seeing New Zealand. Since 1642 many thousands of tourists have exclaimed. New Zealand is that sort of place; 'breathtaking' is almost the right word for once. Ah, New Zealand, land of the long white cloud — or land of the wrong white crowd, as the Maori say.

The Maori killed a couple of Tasman's men when he landed on the north coast of the South Island, but the remainder must have lived well on the mussels. Eventually the explorer went home, gingerless, to his hatchet-faced masters in Batavia who were not sympathetic to his tales of rotten luck in the Antipodes.

Tasman made his landfall just 600 or 700 years after the first Maori arrived. The archaeological story is that before the Maori there were only birds — many of them flightless — and a kind of mouse or rat. The Maori hunted the birds; some of them, like the mighty moa, to extinction.

The moa grew to three or four metres. It was a bird-like Justin Madden in form and, like Justin, harmed no one. For hundreds of years the hillscapes of Otago resounded to the thumps of their great splayed feet propelled by giant drumsticks, as they chased the moths and lowflying birds.

What native fauna the Maori allowed to survive the Europeans savaged. Appalled at the lack of four-legged animals and seeing nothing in a parrot, the English imported weasels and stoats which found the birds a delicacy. (In New Zealand you will see the odd dead weasel on the road, but not enough.)

The prince of parrots is the kakapo which resembles a

kitchen tidy. The kakapo does not fly; it stands for long periods, walks up trees and lies about on limbs like a feathery sloth. No wonder the Protestants had no time for the kakapo at all. Now there are only 30 pairs in existence, all of them on Stewart Island.

The South Island of New Zealand may well be the most beautiful place on Earth. It is the Scottish Highlands, the Monaro High Plains, south-west Tasmania, Aireys Inlet, Port Albert on a cold day and Norway rolled into one. And there is no one there, except in places like Christchurch, Dunedin, Invercargill and Nelson.

Outside these places, and a few others like Queenstown which is glorious but inhabited by skiers, there is no one on the South Island — or not so many that you notice them. You can sit by lakes of peerless glory and imagine the trout in them, gaze upon mountains Swiss in size but more surprising, study glaciers in the midst of their moraine, or simply roll down the tussocky hills with only your wife and their sheep as companions — and occasionally a kea, a parrot notorious among skiers but a friend to humanity.

The kea is worth a diversion. Do not be content with the postcard, which in any case represents the bird as black when in reality it is green with puce underwings. The kea inhabits skiers' car parks and the feet of glaciers — anywhere there are cars or expensive items of apparel. With beak and claw it prises rubber off roof racks and out of door jambs. It steals hats and gloves, sandwiches, Lindt chocolate and has even been known to lever corks from champagne bottles. It loathes human folly and pretension. The kea is a fearless patriot and should be the emblem of New Zealand's civil defence.

The people of the South Island of New Zealand can be described, respectfully, as WASPs. Irish Catholics, the statistics show, are about as rare as four-legged animals once were; there are few Maori and few Continentals. Do not go seeking Galliano and croissants in Dunedin.

The people of Dunedin, it is well known, are descended from Free Church Presbyterians of the Scottish Lowlands who, in 1848, built a city of stone to look like Edinburgh, and indeed called it Edinburgh, in Gaelic. It is a good city, particularly for the First Church which all denominations surely admire, the railway station with its stained-glass window trains, and the statue of Burns with his back to the Anglicans.

You must visit Port Chalmers which fortunately does not appear on the tourist maps. Here a grim Presbyterian church, so puritan it does not even have a sign to say what it is, looks eyelessly out over a container terminal — a black blessing on commerce. Here the noted novelist and publisher, John Hooker, spent some years serving his country, before migrating to Australia to become a noted novelist and publisher. Here is the opportunity to buy a bag of fried oysters and eat them while watching feats of New Zealand navigation.

The hinterland of Dunedin, Otago, is not to be missed. It is to be wondered at. Otago should be motored through slowly with a hamper and always with a view to stopping. This is the tussock and lake country.

Like the rest of New Zealand it is alive with sheep, all bursting with health. The romney marsh is common. When newly shorn the romney looks a bit like a bull terrier, and one can only hope that it will soon replace that species in the inner suburbs of Wellington. Unfortunately for dwellers in Glebe and Carlton, the breed is prone to footrot in Australia.

Christchurch, by contrast to its neighbour in the south, is English and almost inordinately proud of it. Cambridgeish to be more precise. A shallow stream with many ducks upon it flows between ivy-clad university and park. Joggers, cyclists and bookworms abound in the feeble sun. Christchurch is genteel as its founders envisaged. Wakefieldians, they imagined a social order and that is what they got.

There are two places the tourist should not miss in Christchurch. The first is a six-figure World War I memorial by the cathedral. Four of the figures are magnificent, if not burly, women and the other two, representing 'youth' and 'valour', are men — slender men with fine cheekbones and hair neatly parted who look as though they would have been at home in Brideshead.

The best view of Christchurch — and this is the second place you must go — is from the Port Hills on a smog-free day. On the other side there is an even better view of Lyttelton Harbour, a fabulous caldera connected to the sea. Go at dusk to the monument up there which was erected to the memory of the first English women who climbed the hills from the harbour and gazed with understandable awe at the splendour of their new home on the Canterbury Plain. White New Zealand honoured women in a way that Australia never dreamed of.

The other towns to be recommended in the general Canterbury/Otago area are Cromwell and Twizel — God knows who Twizel was. These are hydro towns with cheap motels. Twizel (or is it Cromwell?) is soon to be drowned in a dam, so there is a certain pang to a visit there.

And then there is Arrowtown — what a name. This is quite simply and without qualification a beautiful place. An old gold town, Arrowtown, it has to be said, makes Maldon took like a modern slum. Head into the mountains from Arrowtown and you could well come across a true New Zealander. Far from the pressures of life in a Wellington or a Twizel, Herbert McAlpine has lived all his long life with his animals — sheep and dogs mainly.

'Ths's gd ship country,' says Herbert. 'Gd dg country too.'

'I see,' I say.

Herbert is Otago rural representative of Men Against Pornography, a powerful organisation based in Wellington with a telephone tree extending well into the provinces. You might wonder how pornography can concern a man in the New Zealand semi-wilderness.

'A lot of their corruption blows up here in a southerly,' Herbert says. 'I've been slapped in the face by a *Playboy* centrefold more than once when I've been out after weasels.

They come off the Russian trawlers I reckon, some perhaps from the Australians down at Mawson.'

As you travel around New Zealand you will find yourself asking why the people are so morally upright. Is it because all the loose ones have migrated to Australia? The New Zealanders I spoke to did not seem to know. A motel keeper claimed the question was misguided.

'I'm a liberal,' he said. 'Live and let live. If people want to burn in Hell that's their business.'

Some political scientists put it down to the Protestant ethic and an 'isolation factor', which of course they do not explain. It is argued that the steady decline in rugby union reflects a new generation's rejection of the old rigid morality. They look forward to the day when New Zealand will be less hung up.

If this is so it is a great pity. In New Zealand issues are treated with refreshing moral seriousness and attention to the facts. The journalists, by and large, are not fatuous poll-watchers or hyenas. Policy is actually reported and with little of the punditry which makes Australian newspapers so tiresome. What is more, the New Zealand Government does have a policy.

'We are about moral policy and always have been,' says a councillor from Invercargill. 'We got it from the Kirk. We are all, in one way or another, akin to the old elders of the church. We are like them in stature, demeanour and *weltenschauung* or *tursuinn an cruinne,* as they might have put it. We go red easily when indoors or in trains, being more at ease in the wind and rain. We are not big on restaurants. We have taken much from the Scottish foremothers and fathers,' he says thoughtfully. 'Except perhaps their randiness. No, I don't think we are as randy as they were.'

We did not have time to seek opinion in Fiordland, where the rainfall exceeds 300 inches (7500 mm) per annum.

A woman of Golden Bay, the sunniest spot of the south, explained her position while netting some herring for tea.

'New Zealand,' she said, 'is a small and comfortable country grown suddenly poor. In these circumstances, I tell my husband, it is important not to be ashamed — not like those blighters who clear out to Australia. Sold out their birthright, more interested in Mr Hawke than our David who has resolutely told the French where to go and who is twice, nay, four times the man Hawke is.

'They live on fat Australian salaries, eating *gado gado* and spaghetti — good riddance I feel like saying to them. But it's high time they remembered their homeland and came back and paid for the good education we gave them.'

They can get quite angry in New Zealand, quite patriotic, even in a city like Wellington where the daily paper is called *The Dominion*. Wellington is a hard city — and let me make this clear at once, it is on the *North* Island, the south of the North Island. It blows a gale in Wellington once a week at least. The wind whistles round the weatherboard corners and through the moustaches of the men, creating an eerie comb-and-paper effect.

Wellington is a higgledy-piggledy city sitting on a major fault line which, last time it convulsed, created the present airport runway. Yet the people of Wellington show no sign of fear. Nor do they have pretensions, except perhaps at netball and canoeing in which they excel.

It is true that the Speaker of the National Parliament has a lambswool underblanket on his chair, but this is more an expression of nationalism than a personal affectation, a fact made plain by the yellowed wig he wears.

See New Zealand. See it for the views. Take a mudbath if you must. But see it also for its people who, mercifully immune to modern narcissism, go about their business without seeing themselves.

See it also for Fail's Fish Cafe in Christchurch where the service and the decor will remind you of what Melbourne restaurants might have been. And see it for the kakapo, the parrot king, and a bird of very long memory.

Vincent Buckley

FROM *MEMORY IRELAND*

Now that the struggle in the six northern counties is so advanced, and the ties between Irish and British governments so strong and complex, if rarely visible, coming into Ireland can be fraught with prohibitions. In 1981, when I had been living there already for seven months, and had paid three months' rent in advance to live in marvellous working conditions in County Kildare, I set off to go to an international writers' conference, organised for Amnesty International, in Toronto; there I was to give two papers and a poetry reading. My chosen route took me through Heathrow, my contact with English soil being limited to the bus ride from Terminal 1 to Terminal 3. Trouble arose only when I passed through the immigration desk to catch the Canadian flight. The smart young interrogator wanted to know where in England I would be living on my return and, when I told him I would be going straight to Ireland, became very 'concerned', consulted a book on the desk (*How to Look Concerned? Keep Them in Their Place?*) and a computer list of terrorists, prohibited persons and, no doubt, Irish-Australian poets, suspended under the desk. Then, in spite of my growing impatience, and not meeting my eyes, he stamped the passport briskly and said, 'Report to the Irish authorities in Dublin.' 'What does your stamp say?' I asked. 'I have given you permission to stay in the UK for twenty-one days,' he said. 'But what has that to do with Ireland?' I asked. 'It also entitles you to stay in Air for twenty-one days,' he said; and then the row started, and he had to meet my eyes.

But it was all legal, as in my furious astonishment I

found out; because of those barely visible ties between governments, an English immigration officer can determine the length of my stay in Ireland. I was told the same thing by a much nicer version of the original interrogator as I passed through immigration at Heathrow on my way home to Kildare. 'What Irish authorities?' I said. 'I'm living in Ireland. You've had a fortnight to check up with the Kildare police on whether my wife and children, my rented house and my unpaid bills, are where I said I left them. Just whom are you asking me to see, and why?' 'The Irish immigration officers,' he said. 'Have you ever flown to Dublin?' I said. No. Of course not. 'Immigration officers don't meet English flights,' I said. 'They're rarer than hen's teeth at the airport.' To the 'authorities' in Dublin Castle, then; he would give me a phone number. Special Branch, is it, I said. I imagine so, he said.

I prepared myself to 'report' to the Dublin interrogators in that seat of ancient foreign (English) power, Dublin Castle, now an administrative centre for the Irish Republic, which itself is known incorrigibly to British bureaucrats as 'Air'. Eventually I did; and I was put in touch with a superintendent whose sense of the drama and urgency of my case was so underdeveloped that in the end he seemed more interviewed than interviewing. When asked what legislation it was that required me, an Irishman born in Australia and an Australian national, to accept Irish residence at the say-so of an Englishman, he courteously murmured something about 'alien registration'. 'But almost all my forebears were Irish,' I said. 'I can't possibly regard myself as an alien in this country.' 'Yes,' he said, for, unlike the Englishman, he could see some humour in it all, and thought Necessity the mother of Procrastination. 'I can see it makes you sound like a little green man.' 'I *am* a little green man,' I said.

None of the Irish seemed to feel any sense of urgency about my registering with them, but I came to the conclusion that I had better do it if I were to have a clear passage into England later that year; when I came to register, the grain of conscription in the Irish casualness came out, and I was asked for our passports, which would be returned to me later. 'When?' 'About six weeks.' 'How?' 'By mail.' 'Certainly not,' I said, for I had started to have weekly confrontations with the Irish mail system, 'nobody will be given possession of my passports. If you want to register me, do it now.' And they did, with as much ungracious impersonality as they could muster, which was not much, for the Irish may make you wait for an hour, but it upsets them to have you sitting there for a day (unless they have forgotten all about you, that is).

Anyway, in 1955 all that was a long way in the future, and I was having very few dealings with officialdom. The aim was to scrape by, and we had very little money for amenities. Our general style was one of poverty, and our general ethos was make-do. No university or other institution financed my trips to the places about which I was to write so much; I was offered no free trips, I knew no wealthy individuals who had the makings of hosts for a married poet the lining of whose overcoat was hanging in tatters, and of course I had no 'private means', those resources which have a habit of becoming public, even ostentatious, as soon as you have enough of them. Therefore, we had to choose rooms very carefully, and give some thought to cafés, and consider a little cautiously where to move on to, and when. There was no question of renting cars, and we would not look for ways of 'living off the country'.

The first day of my first trip to Dublin, I left our belongings in the B and B place we had chosen in Portobello (these B and B places have a strange and reassuring resemblance to one another, perhaps because so many of them were built in the same era, and the women who run them seem to come from a common family, with marked religious opinions), and I went for a walk up South Circular Road. Phlegm capital of the world. And at least in the final judging for turds capital, too. I passed Collins Barracks, named for the famous organiser and guerrilla fighter, Michael Collins, and there I had a random, crazy thought, I wonder if Sean O'Faolain is in the phone book, for I had been reading *The*

Bell and thought him in his own way a great and admirable freedom fighter. Into the phone booth, and sure enough he was in the book. I then did something I had never done before, and have never done since, I rang an eminent writer who was a complete stranger.

A woman answered, seemed uncertain what to do, said, 'O I'll see if he's in. We've just come back from the races.' When O'Faolain came to the phone, he said, 'Vincent Buckley. Your name suggests that you're Irish, and your voice suggests that you're English. What are you?' 'Australian,' I said, laughing. Ah. It was all done as easily as writing a cheque, and we met next day to spend the afternoon in the lounge of the Shelbourne, where he drank Dubonnet and looked cosmopolitan in tweeds, while I drank whiskey and gurgled Gaelic salutations. What interested me was not so much his agreeing to meet an unknown and unimportant person (for the Irish, while they are contemptuous of 'chancers', are taken with the unusual), but the fact that he enquired so acutely about Australia. He wanted to know about Australian writing, the theatre, the universities; but most of all he wanted (after having shrewdly sounded me out) to know about Catholic Action, Santamaria, Mannix, the Labor split, and how civil liberties in Australia and in the Catholic church would be affected by recent upheavals. Since his standpoint on these matters was pretty much my own, a good time was had by all. I have never seen him since, and am grateful to him for letting me know that for some Irishmen Australia mattered as a place of discourse and cultural experiment, not simply as a setting for odd holidays or a haven in which you could forget Ireland and make a lot of money.

'Arriving is almost as hard', says my poem. As hard as what? As leaving, for one thing. To leave a country like Ireland is peculiarly hard, and 'leave' means something different from 'leaving' America. You leave New York or San Francisco, any one of the great opposites; but leaving Ireland from any point you feel you are leaving the whole; for everything is so close together, reinforcing everything else on the mind's retina. The fifties were a period of high and poignant emigration, and a great deal of it was to England, Wales or Scotland, often to virtual disappearance in an environment so different from the place of origin, but often to establish a base from which the migrant's relationship to Ireland would be that of hungry revenant: never again totally the son or daughter, never the mere expatriate either, but the person of two homes, the lost and the chosen. It is impossible to overstress the ambivalence of all this, for Britain had in many cases come to be chosen.

At that time I travelled always on the mailboat, from Holyhead to Dun Laoghaire or Liverpool to Dublin; and I can report without undue sentimentality that, each time, it was concertinas home and bitter silence back. More than once I saw people dancing and singing, on deck or in the saloon, in the middle of the Irish Sea; but it was always *en route* to Ireland. On the way back to Britain to what was technically or really home for most of the travellers, I never heard one note of equable music. At the time I romantically thought this psychic arrangement apt; now I find it quite strange. Yet, then, many of the travellers were seriously disoriented, not even remotely up to re-orienting themselves in a new country. A Melbourne taxi-driver, a Wicklow man, told me that when he left home, at sixteen, he carried a few pound notes rolled up inside his shoe; by the time he got to Cricklewood, they had disintegrated. Yet the thought was good; it was the prior briefing that was defective. More than once I gave lifts in a taxi to young people whose cousins or brothers had failed to meet them at Euston. The Legion of Mary had volunteers boarding every ship to see to the worries of departing migrants, but they could not adequately oversee them at the point of arrival. The Irish were like seeds cast into a furrow but blown by a foreign wind into marsh or ditch; there was a limit to what anyone could do for them. Older migrants, including people in their twenties, men in the 'building trade', men and women in 'the catering trade' or 'service', sat waiting for the boat train calm, purposeful, sad.

In July 1957, the day after a mass internment of republicans, picked up in hundreds after a series of police sweeps, the boat we were taking back to Liverpool was full of depressed women and agitated children. I was reading *The United Irishman*, and some of them started talking to me. They were the families of republicans, going for safety to their relations in England.

Another time, having a drink in the bar, I noticed a great tall Donegalman drinking, and singing 'Brennan on the Moor'. I remember his overcoat trailing. Half an hour later I came back, and he was fighting five men, three of whom were trying to clap him in irons. I was standing next to a wondering Englishman, who turned out to be a sales rep., or travelling salesman, as they were called in those days. 'What happened?' I said. 'I don't know,' he said. 'One minute he was singing, and the next he and his mate were trying to kill each other.' Actually, they looked like brothers, thus making the scenario more logical.

The arrivals at Dun Laoghaire at 6 am should be disconsolate, for if it's not cold it's wet, but the arriving travellers bustle off to somewhere they want to reach. If you are waiting, to meet someone, you feel like an animal hiding in a world of darkness which is furtive and scared and may itself be animal. But the spirit is one of fulfilment. And arrivals by air, however bizarre or sloppily arranged they may be in detail, can be counted on to have panache. On one occasion, flying into Shannon from Montreal, with the schedules mixed up in some way, I found myself with an overcrowded plane some hours late, and the hostesses flustered almost into incoherence. We bucketed across Ireland from west to east, at a height that seemed a couple of thousand feet, performing to an audience of every creature that lived on the island and was capable of looking up: speed, rocketing; object, to reduce lateness; demeanour of cabin crew, agitated and extraordinarily sweet; demeanour of my neighbours, gabby, self-revelatory, a little polemical (against dole bludgers): 'Well, we can't all work in the Bank of Ireland,' I said. 'I work in the Allied Irish actually,' said my nearest neighbour. 'But you must admit I'm right. You have the same in your own country,' she said triumphantly (for she had spent six weeks in Sydney). At any moment I expected a cow or a pig to point upward and cry out; you could see the shadow of the plane crossing them. It was all green, and very beautiful, and varied, and ad hoc, and there was nothing portentous about it at all.

Bernard Smith
FROM *THE BOY ADEODATUS*

'I love coming here,' said the insurance man to Mum Keen one day, as he stood under the tall loquat by the back door. 'So cool and restful. You've made it look so beautiful. It's like the garden of Eden. All you need is Adam and Eve.' And gave young Bertha a sly look.

Little Bennie didn't like him. A bit of a flash Jack. Each week he picked up the sixpences on the industrial policies that Mum Keen had taken out on Bertha's life and then on Ben's.

He never forgot that day.

'What's his name?' the insurance man said to Bertha, who was standing shyly by the back door, her long hair hanging down to her waist. She loved her hair.

'Bernard William Smith,' she said.

'Then he's not one of the family,' he said.

'No,' she said.

'He's not one of yours,' he said with a sly smile.

'Of course not,' she said blushing. 'His mother's gone to Queensland.'

'Oh, he's one of those,' he said.

Bertha, still blushing, said nothing. But little Bennie knew what the man meant. He had always seemed to know; and to know was to know the world. To know everything. *And now behold, my infancy is dead . . . yet I live still.*

In the summer the garden was full of fruit: figs, and pomegranates, which made your teeth black, passionfruit and grapes. Bert's grass lawn was sprinkled with falling plums much visited by bees. That was Bennie's first memory, vivid and painful. Climbing under the string fence onto the newly planted grass, and then the sting as the pain shot through his body. How he yelled.

'Oh Mum,' cried Bertha, 'little Bennie's trodden on a bee.' Out came Mum Keen, quick as lightning from her wash-tub, the Reckitt's blue in her hand; and dabbed it on his throbbing toes.

But an even more disturbing thing happened in the garden, when Eric came back from Mittagong. 'Eric's a good boy really,' Mum Keen said, 'but sometimes the Devil gets into him.'

And one day, not long after Bennie had learned to walk and was trying to sweep up some autumn leaves with the small broom old Dad had given him, the Devil did get into Eric. Suddenly he shot out of the back door, like a startled rabbit, with Mum Keen after him — a broomstick high above her head. Round and round the house they went, to a rustle of falling leaves. Down the side by the Carradice fence, past the dwarf fuchsia bush, the ferns and the palm trees, the small red meter that always smelt slightly of escaping gas; and out across the front garden, up by the Meares's fence; then round and round again. Like a streak of lightning Eric went.

Ben never knew what it was that the Devil made Eric do when it got into him; and could never remember whether Mum Keen ever caught Eric or gave him a hiding. But the vision of flying Eric struck a dull terror into his heart. Naughty boys went to Mittagong or away up north to milk cows, and never came back. He did not see Eric again until Eric was a man.

During the late summer Ben helped Bertha and Valerie pick the plums. Baskets and baskets of them. Bertha held the ladder while Ben climbed up with a basket. 'Don't play the fool, or you will fall,' Bertha said. Then Mum Keen would begin to make pots and pots of jam: plum, marmalade, melon and lemon. She bought big pale melons from the Burwood Fruit Mart and they all sat down around the white deal table in the back veranda, cutting the melon first into long slices, then into chunky little blocks. Mum Keen would scrape it all into a great iron saucepan on the top of the fuel range. When it was cooked and had cooled, about a hundred jars were filled with a wooden spoon and the tops sealed with candle wax. Valerie and Ben would wait for a lick of the wooden spoon from the last scrapings of the pot. The jars of jam lasted through the year and also served Mum Keen as thank-you presents for her Burwood ladies.

Valerie came to Burwood because one day Mum Keen said to Bertha, 'I think Ben needs a little companion.' So one night they all went off in the train to Lidcombe. And then walked to an old timber house falling to one side in which there lived an old lady with two small boys. There were two big greyhounds, straining and snapping in their kennels. And there was little Val.

'We will have to get you another dress,' said Mum Keen as they came back in the train. Val was two years older than Ben. She was given a bed on the back veranda in a corner closed in by heavy shutters that had been painted chocolate-brown.

Some would say that the Keens were poor. But they never thought of themselves as poor. The children in that house were never hungry. Old Dad managed the vegetable patch: cabbages and carrots, parsnips and beans. A big stand of rhubarb flourished by the garden tap, watered by constant dripping. Jerusalem artichokes grew along the Meares's fence. All the Keens had green fingers.

'You can start your little garden here with radishes, Ben,' said old Dad, standing by the fowl-run. 'They grow quickly if you keep watering them.' So Ben put in some seeds and was so anxious to watch them grow that he would get up early in the morning and stir the soil with his fingers just to see if the roots were swelling.

Mum Keen had saved and saved to put down a deposit on Braeside. 'Look after the pennies,' she said, 'and the pounds will look after themselves.' But old Dad was never much interested in the pennies or the pounds. His Bible, constantly by his side, told him not to worry about money. It was harder, he said, for a rich man to enter into the kingdom of heaven than for a camel to pass through the eye of a needle, and he showed Ben where it was written down in the Bible. A proud family who kept their own counsel.

But Mum Keen possessed no pride when it came to a bit of manure for the garden. She seemed to know by the look in the horse's eye, Jack Carns, who was a real dag, would say. And there she would be with her hand broom and coal scuttle almost before the milkman's horse had dropped it. Not the sort of thing that Mrs Meares or Mrs Larter would be seen doing. But they liked and admired Tottie Keen, though they thought she was a bit of a queer one with her garden always full of leaves, and State kids of all ages popping in and out of the house.

In the Carradice corner of the yard the Keens kept a few chooks. Bert had wired it in and built a roost, roofing it over with some old scraps of tin, then run some wire netting around a lemon tree up to the back fence. Mum Keen kept Black Orpingtons because they were good layers and she liked their large brown eggs. There were some White Leghorns too and some bantams. The bantam rooster was a little beauty with the sun shining on his feathers, crimson and gold; a real scream to watch, strutting up to the great old Black Orpington cock, with one leg high in the air, his neck hunched forward and all his feathers ruffled up; as proud and cocky as a governor-general.

In the winter all the couch grass in Bert's lawns turned brown and died back. Old Dad began to do the pruning and trenching. It was Doodie who showed Ben how to trench: up to the neck of the spade and the earth well over. Now the great Japanese plum was just a bundle of sticks in the sky; and you could see the parapets of the shops along Burwood Road standing up between the bare branches. At either end of one parapet stood two big urns shaped with little spikes like German helmets on top. Winter and summer they were there, but in the summer they were hidden by leaves. They fascinated Ben. At night they stood out blackly against the deep-blue sky, and could be seen clearly on a moonlit night, or in a storm, all white, when lit suddenly by a flash of lightning. Why were they there like clocks sounding the hours?

At Braeside the kitchen was the busy centre of the house. Mum Keen, a good plain cook, presided over her fuel range. Sago puddings and bread and butter custards were her specialities. Roasts with golden roast potatoes on the weekend, if things were going well. Bertha never cooked. When money was short they ate rabbit. Out Mum Keen would go with her tin dish to the cry of 'Rabbito' and come back with a pair, the black blood from their mouths spreading in the dish. There were many cries in Esher Street in those times. Swiss yodelling was a fashion. 'Any, any milk today; only fourpence ha'penny a quart I say,' the milkman would cry. He was the best yodeller in Burwood. Out Ben and Val would run with a jug and he would pour a quart from a tap in the back of his cart, while the horse stamped on the ground and flicked the flies off his rump with his tail. Then they would go back in and report any sightings of fresh manure.

It was the Chinese hawkers that Mum Keen liked best. They're hard workers, she would say, and they always have a smile for you. One old Chinaman, with two heavy bamboo baskets balanced at the end of a long bamboo rod, sold only pots of ginger. But what Bertha and Mum Keen loved most were visits from the Chinaman who sold silks and satins. Out they would come, one after another, from a large old cardboard suitcase that seemed to have no bottom. He would spread his pretty treasures over everything in the back veranda; the tables and chairs, the ferns and the pots of aspidistra, and then spread them over the floor until the place began to glow like an eastern bazaar. A case without a bottom, like something magic out of the *Arabian Nights*. Always he kept smiling gently at Mum Keen, as he pulled out more and more splendid things, murmuring quietly but with great conviction, as in an incantation or a prayer, 'Something pretty, very pretty for your daughter.' Occasionally Mum Keen bought some little thing, because she never could resist a bargain. But it was the occasion that she adored.

Mum Keen was a careful manager. Ten shillings came into the house weekly from old Dad's pension from the State Brickworks; 10s each for Valerie and Ben, and 10s rent from any young lodger who might be there. The rest of the Braeside income came from taking in washing. But the garden produced so much that they were partly self-supporting in eggs, fruit and vegetables. Even so Mum Keen had to be thrifty. Valerie never saw a dress of her own in the seven years that she lived at Braeside. Either Bertha's old dresses, or dresses from the daughters of Mum Keen's Burwood ladies. But little Bennie did get new clothes when they felt he needed them because he was a bit of a pet in that house; and Mumma Parky sent some money down for clothes from Queensland when she could afford it. Whenever Mum Keen felt he was in need of a new outfit she would take him in the train to Central Station, then catch the tram down to Bon Marche store at the corner of Parramatta Road and Harris Street, Ultimo. It was there, she said, that you got good quality at a fair price. Once a year she took Bennie to a big building in the city. Up they would go to the seventh floor in the big iron lift, like monkeys in a cage. After waiting for a time on a long bench, they would go into a room where a man sat behind a large desk. Mum Keen always went over and talked to the man and Ben couldn't hear what they said; and when he sometimes did, he still couldn't understand. Then the man would turn to him and say always the same thing.

'Do you like your home, Ben?' Smiling sheepishly at him, knowing what the answer would be. 'Always be a good boy, Ben, and you will get on well,' he would say as they left the room.

But Ben didn't have to be told that, because he remembered Eric flying round and round the house and Mum Keen after him with the broomstick. He sometimes wondered where Eric had gone. But the man in the big building was kind and Ben was not afraid of him. *O God, my God! what miseries and what mockeries did I find in that age; whenas being yet a boy, obedience was propounded unto me, to those who advised me to get on in the world.*

Little Bennie always sat for his meals on the long brown form that was placed beneath the kitchen window behind the table. Outside the small red fuchsia bloomed through the summer in all its glory. It was Mum Keen's greatest pride, and the admiration of her Burwood ladies as they came to collect their washing or sit down for a chat and cup of tea. At the end of the table by the stove sat old Dad. A man who never raised his hand in anger. If one of Tottie's State kids sometimes annoyed him, the most he would do was to swing his hand over the top of the boy's head, lightly touching his hair. George Keen left the management of the household to his wife, and she thought him a bit of a fool at times; but she had great faith in his powers of healing. If you had a headache all you had to do was to kneel down between old Dad's knees and he would place his scarred and horny brickworker's hands on either side of your head, just touching the temples ever so softly. The laying on of hands. The warmth seemed to go through your body; the headache went away. No one was ever known, at any rate, to say that their headache hadn't gone away. 'I don't know whether it's his electricity or whether it's God,' Mum Keen would say, 'but it always works.'

Old Dad kept all the shoes at Braeside in good repair. Up in the back shed he kept his father's old boot last. It had three sides: one for a man-size boot, one for a lady's shoe, and one for a heel. On the wall nearby hung a length of good quality calf's hide leather. Whenever their boots or shoes required mending he would put on his leather apron, sharpen his fine pocket knife, which he greatly treasured, on his whetstone, and then sit to his last. Little Ben would watch fascinated as with strong hands he cut round the edge of the shoe, an even oblique stroke, as clean as through butter, then moulded the edges with crisp cuts of his sharp knife. Last of all he would nail the new sole on with small brass tacks.

When Ben first came to Braeside he was an infant, and he slept for a few months in the marriage bed of Mum Keen and old Dad: a big iron double bed, a half-tester, with brass foot pillars and porcelain spindles. Later they gave him a cot. There he lay in a great sweat with the measles, the design in the curtain, from which he could not take his eyes, coming at him like a fierce cat with its claws, then whirling around faster and faster. One night, when he was better, old Dad gave him a small book with a brown cover. It had coloured pictures in it.

'I will teach you to read from this book,' old Dad said, 'because it is the best book in the world.' Much later, after he had learned to read, old Dad said, 'Now you must promise me to read two chapters every night before you go to sleep.' And that he did, two chapters every day from the age of six to the age of thirteen, except when sick. He developed a great love of the stories in the Old Testament: of Joseph, of the children of Israel released from bondage in Egypt, of the young Samuel, and especially the book of Daniel, with that wonderful story of Shadrach, Meshach and Abednego, who would not bow down to the golden image of the king and were not consumed by the fiery furnace. The illustrations in the Bible haunted his imagination for years. One was of a city, and under it were written the words 'A city without walls cannot be hid'. It troubled him. Sydney was a city without walls. How could it hide itself from the curious, questioning, all-seeing eye of God?

One day old Dad said, 'Make up a list of the words you know, Ben.' He must have known about thirty at that time. But he was proud of his Biblical knowledge and searched the Bible for the biggest word he knew. So after a string of mat, fat and sat words, after Peter the kookaburra and Mumbo the cat, and Valerie, came Nebuchadnezzar, though for a long time he pronounced it *knee bucket sneezer.*

On the opposite side of the kitchen table from old Dad sat Jeff, a quiet man, always doing crossword puzzles. Jeff was very important because he had just come back from the Front, where he had been gassed a bit, and was a little bit shell-shocked. But he wouldn't talk about the war. You could read his name on the new memorial arch they were building in Burwood Park; Clarence Jeffrey, inscribed on a grey marble slab with the names of all the returned boys, in silver. If you were killed in the war and did not come back they put your name up there in gold. One large panel was full of gold names. Little Ben liked Jeff, who taught him to do crossword puzzles and gave him books to read. He never got angry, except once. But then he got very angry.

After returning from the war Jeff began to learn a trade — french-polishing. Chairs and tables with delicate joinery would appear in the back shed at various stages of sanding, staining and polishing. Now one of the Braeside pets, which Mum Keen had picked up somewhere, was a galah that talked a lot. They put him in a cage that could be moved from tree to tree. One unhappy day little Ben moved that cage up near the back shed and left it quite close to one of Jeff's highly polished antique chairs. It must have contained a kind of varnish that galahs relish because by mid-morning Cocky, sticking his head through his cage, had eaten deeply into a corner of a cabriole leg. When Jeff came out to give his chair a final rubdown of wax and polish he found that a great part of the shoulder of one leg had been eaten away. He flew into a wild rage, while the wretched bird, delighted to have some personal attention, jumped up and down on his perch, first on one leg, then on the other, screeching, 'Scratch Cocky, scratch Cocky.'

'Scratch be damned, you fucking bird,' said Jeff, 'that's no scratch, you've just about eaten the bloody thing up, you've buggered up my chair. What stupid fool put the mad galah there.'

Bennie kept well out of Jeff's way for days. Shortly afterwards Jeff and old Dad built a permanent aviary for the galah and the love birds, under the big Japanese plum.

Jeff was the only boy from Braeside to join the AIF and go to France. Mum Keen wouldn't let her sons go because she didn't believe in war. But when they all came back the patriotic fever gripped Braeside as it gripped the rest of the country. On Sunday evenings they would gather round the piano in the dining room, which was hardly ever used for dining, even at Christmas. It was the best room in the house, only used when very special visitors came, or for Sunday evening get-togethers. On these occasions Bertha would play a few hymns first from the Moody and Sankey or Anderson hymnals. Then she would play 'The Rose of Picardy' or 'When the Boys Come Marching Home' and end up with 'It's a Long Way to Tipperary'. Bertha's music certificate, the primary examination of the London College of Music, which she had passed on 23 November 1914 at the age of twelve, was framed above the bamboo music case. But after that Mum Keen couldn't afford to pay for any further lessons from Miss Marion Anderson, the local music teacher. On very special evenings Bertha would place candles in the brass sconces of her Beale piano and they would all gather around her and sing hymns by the candlelight, and popular songs to satisfy the boys.

It was a well-furnished room for a family of such modest means; evidence enough of Tottie Keen's desire to identify herself with the respected members of Burwood's community. But into it, through the heavy curtains, the daylight rarely penetrated. In the centre of the room stood a heavy extension table, darkly varnished and covered with a thick rust-brown velvet cloth, which was never removed except occasionally to dust. Around the table were ten Austrian cane bentwood chairs — strong, light, easy to move about. To one side of the table stood Bertha's piano and on the other the rosewood sideboard that held the family tableware: silver-plated coffee pots and salvers, and a soup tureen in late Victorian rococo, heavily moulded, a pink glass biscuit barrel, and a fruit dish in open-latticework porcelain of which Mum Keen was very proud. They must have come to her from her mother after she died at Marrickville in 1903. In the centre of the sideboard stood that most precious family shrine, the three top tiers of the Keens' wedding cake, entombed in domed glass on a velvet base. The tiny columns of icing sugar still held their lintels and cornices as firmly as when Mr Blair, Burwood's finest cake man and confectioner, had first put them all together. The sugar sprigs of orange still sprouted and blossomed, the sugar flags fluttered, and sugar birds flew in the timeless air, as they did on that day when Tottie Davis married George Keen, not for love but, as she always said, for old times' sake. As a young girl Bertha dusted the glass dome each week with loving care. But after Mum Keen died, and the remaining members of the family lived more than ever in the kitchen, the dome gathered dust and mildew in the darkened room.

There was less singing around the piano after Bert bought his phonograph. It had a long horn and little cylindrical records that were kept in a big flat wooden box lined with felt and stored in the back shed. The voices sounded faint and scratchy. The one that little Bennie remembered best began 'O the moon shines bright on pretty Red-wing'. But the kids down the street sang other words.

O the moon shines bright on Mrs Porter,
And on her daughter.
They wash their feet in soda water.

Funny how kids made up silly words to songs. It had to make you laugh; and sometimes it could make you mad. Doodie, who was always good for a lark, knew how to make little Ben mad. He would just have to start singing:

I met with Napper Tandy and he took me by the hand,
And he said how poor old Ireland was,
And how she does stand.

And Ben would run at him and start hitting him with his little fists. 'Stop singing that song, Dood.' Then Dood would say, 'Don't get your Irish paddy up, Ben. It's just a song.'

But little Bennie didn't like that song because he knew what it meant. It meant that he wasn't really one of them; and he wanted to be one of them. *For I was but flesh, a wind that passeth away and cometh not again.*

Anna-Maria Dell'oso

The Softening of Blows

She was born at the precise moment when the full August moon bore down on the night sky to give way to the sun. I was already at the airport, bundled in an overcoat, clutching a hastily packed overnight bag. A handful of people in the East-West lounge read magazines or sat with their eyes half-closed. Wind and stars pressed against the terminal's glass; outside the first dawn planes whined and screamed to be released. On the tarmac, I saw the moon hang as huge as a pregnant belly. It trembled and spilled as the sun slowly pierced the sky.

By the time the plane arrived in the cold high-country town of Armidale, New South Wales, I was a godmother. My girlfriend was delivered of a daughter at 6.35 am at Armidale Hospital, assisted by her husband, her thirteen-year-old daughter and the baby's godfather. I had missed the birth by nearly two hours. It seemed I was the only friend without that silent force-field, an energy one can almost smell, that surrounds people who have seen a creature born. I was envious and a little disappointed, for I was the baby's godmother. I had my wishes to bestow and I had arrived later than the thirteenth fairy.

A week before, I had collected a few days off and flown to Armidale to wait. Any day the baby would arrive. The baby's mother moved as distant as a ship in the ocean, negotiating the cliffs of supermarket aisles and hardware counters. Everything around her seemed suspended, becalmed. She seemed to have been pregnant forever and it felt as though nothing could change. The baby was a pure thin concept in my imagination, as difficult to truly feel as spring in the middle of winter or hunger after a hearty meal. The baby's godfather and I peeled vegetables, placing the phone on the kitchen table. Everywhere we moved, the cord would extend and retract after us. The baby clung to its own cord and bided its time.

After a week, I was forced to return home. The last I heard of the baby was through a stethoscope, the muffled sound of a creature galloping under water. Perhaps the baby was waiting for the full moon, for the right time and tide. It was many scientifically uncalculated weeks later that I held my goddaughter for the first time. Too new to have a name, she seemed like a sea creature washed up from an ancient beach. Water-wrinkled, her face crawled with tiny puckers and sighs and her eyes opened and shut like clams, emitting an intense wet blue light.

Fate had chosen me as her godmother but what did this mean? Lately, another of my girlfriends had given birth in Canada and I found myself godmother to a baby boy. We career-minded girls who avoided the first marriage-and-babies rush after university were now approaching thirty with its strange, profound changes. Was the godmother a quaint role like a bridesmaid or a matron-of-honour? My girlfriends were all post-feminist and unsentimental, yet the choosing of the godmother (and godfather) was an inexplicably necessary ritual. It was moving to be chosen. The fairytales began to haunt my mind, for on some dreamy level I understood them for the first time.

I watched the baby, trying to read the flickering expressions that crossed her face, as though I was a gypsy reading tea-leaves. The mother's all-absorbing, fully committed love is not enough. New creatures also need the dispassionate care of the godparent. Why? I think perhaps it is to soften the harsh dictates of fate.

In the fairytales, the thirteenth fairy is the one left out of the celebrations. She is the unseen and uninvited one. No one thinks of her in the midst of joy. Who wants to see that ugly old crone, Fate, dressed in her grim rags of reality, pain and sadness? Yet she will turn up at every creature's cradle.

Remembered or not, she will be there, standing at the head of every new possibility and those who fail to at least send her an invitation are liable to incur her wrath.

I feel it is best to be on at least a nodding acquaintance with Fate. Our scientific society with its flow-charts and controlled planning of this, that and the other has forgotten the power of the thirteenth fairy. We are punished for our hubris when she screeches down, all of a black fury, upon the dearest and newest creatures born to us, whether they are people or plans or loves or any creations long and eagerly awaited. Twentieth century Western society has neglected to ask the thirteenth fairy to RSVP perhaps more than any civilisation has ever done. Fate? Balderdash! She was last heard of in a couple of Greek choruses. Fate is now superstitious nonsense banished from her role with all new growth . . . because we control all new growth (or damn well know why). And here is the saving grace of the godmother, the twelfth fairy. Fortunately, the godmother does not speak before Fate lays her curse. The godmother softens the blow, so that instead of the worst possible fate, there is only the sleep of 100 years, another chance, another set of possibilities.

Across from us in the ward, a woman in the first stage of labour is moaning yet observing us with interest. Here with the newborn, the baby's older sister, already proficient in cuddling and burping, sings the theme from 'Dallas' as a lullaby. This big sister is wishing her beauty. The friends who come to crowd around the hospital bed, the feminist pals, the mates, the students and relatives, all wish the baby precious luminous gifts.

Strangely, though I've carefully planned to attend the arrival of my goddaughter, some fate has had me miss the birth. I am almost the last of the well-wishers to see her, late at night after her mother has slept through the day and woken for hospital tea and a quick hairbrush and make-up. There may be those who see the role of godmother as mere traditional frippery like blue wedding garters and 'For She's A Jolly Good Fellow'. I defy them to explain the magic of suddenly understanding you have a spell to cast that no other has seen to give. The softening of blows. As the baby opens and shuts her anemone fingers around my face, I see that against the future terrors of this princess, I have a spiritual power; to mitigate the worst, to step in against the slings and arrows of outrageous fortune.

Tim Winton

GRAVITY

Jerra Nilsam sat with his son at a cafe table and the breeze was in his shirt. The day was gone from him now, and there was a party to attend. To host, in fact. It was a friend's birthday. Today was also the anniversary of his father's death.

With great concentration, the little boy made a handprint with icecream on the glass table, and looking beyond him, Nilsam saw the traffic pass. He had come to love the city. It was no capitulation on his part; merely a gradual awareness of new beauties. He was older now, he felt it.

'Go home, Daddy?'

'In a minute, mate. Let me finish my coffee.'

Wait, little man, he thought. Let me procrastinate a bit more.

The three-year-old's eyes were intent on him. They were black, dark as his hair.

'Pongs?'

'No, you can leave your thongs off if you want. But finish your icecream.'

The child held the dripping cone out to show he had eaten enough. Nilsam took it, licked it once, and upended it in the ashtray.

'Come on, me mate.'

Through the flat streets they rode with the wind in their faces. The boy sat strapped into his seat over the rear wheel with his rubber thongs threaded up his forearms. He shrilled a song Rachel would sing him in the bath in the mornings, the quiet time when Nilsam transcribed with an ear to the sounds of the house.

'Green for go!' cried the boy, beating him on the back.

Nilsam coasted through the lights. The sweat and heat of pedalling made him vibrant.

'Ready for the party?' he yelled back over his shoulder. The boy clapped. Oh, God, the party.

'Yaaa!'

They rattled past parked cars to beat the sunset home.

Their street was always full of cars, but now there were so many there didn't seem to be enough room for houses. As they coasted into the driveway, Jerra heard the music. It was his own music they were playing. His heart contracted.

'Party!' the boy cried. 'Yaay!'

Nilsam got off and wheeled the bike up the leafy side of the house. He had to struggle to counterbalance the child's excited lurching. The sudden light and roar of the packed yard stopped him dead. People, some friends, greeted him. They tickled the boy.

He smelt the thin, cutting edge of tobacco smoke and the subtlest hint of dope. Everywhere was light, in jewellery and bottles and eyes and glasses. He heard his songs, his not-very-famous songs. Food passed him. He saw how trodden the lawn was. He was glad to see the door to his studio padlocked. It was an old shed his father had renovated for him. Rachel turned from where she stood speaking with friends across the courtyard and saw him. He knew there was trouble.

'Some lemonade, Daddy?' the little boy shrilled. 'Loud.' He covered his ears. 'Loud.'

Nilsam leant the bicycle against the paling fence, unstrapped the child and led him to a table where he let him pour himself a drink. Lemonade sloshed onto the hired tablecloth. The boy drank unquietly and smiled around the glass.

'Good?' Nilsam asked. His mouth was dry and a terrible heaviness was in him.

'Marvellous.'

'Where'd you get a word like that?' But the child was drinking again and the bubbles made him giggle.

He felt Rachel at his side. She was tall and slim. Her dark hair was out and she wore a thin cotton dress. Her tan made her look as though she was made from polished jarrah. He was sad.

'Where were you, for God's sake? I thought you must have had an accident.'

'We stayed too long at the Italia. It was cool, wasn't it, Sam? Sorry.' He thought he could smell suntan oil. It was the frangipani in bloom.

'You haven't done a bloody thing for this. Poor Ann thinks you've snubbed her. Philip is drunk —'

'Okay.' She was beginning to cry, it always frightened him. 'What do you want me to do?'

'Oh, Jerra.'

Rachel went inside and left him with the heavy scent of the frangipani and a strange, hurtling sensation. His music jangled out at him. He went across, under the pergola, to the tapedeck, cut the music, pulled out the tape and put something else in, something fashionable.

Philip intercepted him on his way to the back door.

'Modesty strikes him down.' Philip pointed at the cassette in Nilsam's hand.

'Hi, Phil.'

'My wife is offended.'

'And you're drunk. I've heard.'

Philip had got thin these past years. Eight years back he'd married Ann and they'd honeymooned in Jerra's shack on the south coast though it had not been a success. Ann had got fat. Nilsam carried too much weight himself and it had begun to annoy him. Philip looked pasty. His soft, hairless face had the practised vulnerability of the social worker. Jerra liked him, but not tonight.

'Tell her I'm sorry, eh?' Jerra said. He touched Philip on the arm as was expected. 'And tell her she's a silly bitch for getting offended.'

He left Philip with a cheap hurt look on his face and went inside. People fussed in the kitchen. In the laundry, someone broke ice with a hammer. He heard the tail end of a joke. Seats in the living-room were pulled into pairs. Social workers, he thought; more bloody Deep and Meaningfuls. It's a party, for God's sake.

Rachel was in the bedroom. She sat in the big, ugly reading chair with a biography of Martin Luther King across her bare knee. He knew she hadn't been reading.

'You've ruined it.'

'I know,' he said. He saw the mahogany sheen of her folded leg.

'What's the matter with you?'

'I don't know.' He couldn't bring himself to mention his father. ***You should know***, he wanted to bellow. 'I really am sorry.'

Her mouth closed against him. When she did that he could see her age. He picked up a little orange gumboot from the floor.

'He insists on wearing these bloody things all summer,' he said with a weak laugh.

'Where is Sam?'

'I don't know. Out the back somewhere. Probably scoffing the horses' doovers. He'll stink of anchovies tonight. I'll have to sleep in the spare room. Come on. We better go outside and be hosts.'

But out under the party lights of the pergola, his new resolve waned. His smile split his face, his jokes petered out mid-sentence; he couldn't look their friends in the eye. Ann stood with two other women beside a table bristling with bottles. He caught her looking at him, looked away.

You're thirty years old, he told himself; be adult enough to go and smooth things over. He got himself a glass of semillon. He took a few serious breaths. And he stayed where he was. He stood rigid beside Rachel as she spoke with their guests.

This morning he had woken in fear. There was a hole in him. Something was lost from him. It wasn't until the afternoon, when, riding with Sam past *Bill's Bait and Tackle,* he knew. The first anniversary. A thought struck him hard: that tall man in loose grey trousers with that stooped, expectant stance and the big hands so often hairy with pollard, was only a memory. He was dead. Actually, finally, dead. And now there was nothing for Jerra Nilsam to fall against. Riding down that street, Nilsam felt as though he was balancing a bicycle for the first time. For the moment, there was no exhilaration, only gravity.

The party wore on. Bottles emptied and the lawn was flattened with sporadic dancing until, in the middle of it all, someone gagged the stereo and brought out a guitar. A thin, droopy young man began to play 'Stairway to Heaven'. Nilsam groaned. Dancers bitched quietly beneath the frangipani.

'It's 1985, for God's sake,' he muttered. '1973 is over.' Someone shushed him. Someone else tittered.

'Amateurs not good enough for you?' a woman hissed from across the courtyard.

Nilsam found a chair at the end of the garden. He'd wait it out. From there he overheard the same conversations about IVF and planes of consciousness and divorces. After a while, Sam came by, slit-eyed and cranky. He put the child over his knee and put him to sleep with three-quarter-time pats on the back. Under the pergola, Rachel moved dutifully from one faction to the next. The Deep and Meaningfuls whispered, solemn. The Ragers agitated for more dance music. Everyone drank too much. Ann stood sullen by the back door. Philip went to sleep in a deckchair.

Nilsam weathered it out, protected from conversation by the sleeping child.

'Use the brakes, Jerra!' Old man running behind. Tinsel on the lawn. Christmas. Old man holding the back of the seat. Charging around the yard on the reddest bike in the world. And then the grip gone, no old man. Sudden grave feeling of independence. Turning, turning. 'You'll be right!' the old man calls. Then the roses, the thorns, looming. Whooaa!

He woke with a flinch. There was a craziness in his belly, as though he was about to fall. He put his face to the little boy's neck and closed his eyes.

Neither Rachel nor Ann spoke to him when he helped them clean up. He collected bottles and broken glasses, picked up cigarette butts with dramatic disdain, swept, sighed. When they went inside he knew better than to join them. Philip was still asleep in the deckchair. Snoring disfigured his face. Jerra unlocked the studio behind the courtyard, went in and shut the door.

The studio was a foetid, dusty place. The egg cartons on the walls gave it a weird look. There was little room in which to move. The place was full of microphones on stands, cords, a piano, an organ, various guitars, mandolin, banjo, the eight-track recorder, a drum machine, mixing desk, metronome, sheets of paper, bits of carpet and blanket and rickety chairs. Here Nilsam wrote songs and sold them to singers who never quite sang them well enough or in the presence of people influential enough to make him rich. They were not love songs and not particularly sad. Rachel sang them to Sam at bedtime and bathtime, and having her sing them was enough for him to continue. But she never sang in front of him. He had to eavesdrop to hear her husky, wavery voice. The sound of it made his skin prickle.

Rachel and he had met on the beach. It was after he returned from the south, when his mind had cooled enough to set a little and he could see the shape of things and the shapes could be borne. His father was sick by then. It was autumn and he had not been near the sea for a long time. He stood, raw, in the carpark. There was a young woman trying to break into her own car. They got talking. As the smooth, cold swells cast themselves onto the sandbanks with surfers in their bellies, Jerra Nilsam knew this tall, brown woman was important to him. That same day he visited his parents. There was talk between them by now. Out in the sun, the old man pulled the rug across his knees and stared at him with a look of comprehension, as though he recognised some understanding in his son at last. Jerra Nilsam felt his soured adolescence leaving him.

He turned the eight-track on. He listened for a few moments to his doodlings on a keyboard and then he switched it off. For a long time he did nothing but sit in this haven the old man had built for him before he died. It was his father's idea. As soon as Rachel and Jerra were married, the old man came around with his tools. He said he wanted to do it before the cancer beat him down, and besides, if *he* didn't do it, his son never would. Jerra was no handyman.

When he went out into the warm night, Philip was gone from the deckchair and the house was in darkness.

Sam and Rachel were asleep. He slid into bed beside them. He lay a while, listening to their sounds, and the old melancholy took him. He lifted the blind a little so he could see them in the light from the street. Rachel's hair was plaited and thick on the pillow. She slept with her back to him. Sam was face-down between the pillows. He always looked as though he'd fallen asleep crawling.

Rushing back to him in his sadness were those first few seconds of the birth, the awful rending of flesh, the tiny blue slug tossed onto Rachel's belly, the crew snatching him away to work on that sunken little chest, and Jerra's first words of prayer since childhood.

Letting go the blind, he fell back onto his pillow, and as often happened now, the memory of Sam suffering into life caused him to weep and shake until he thought he would wake the others. That hiccuping little chest, the pink froth, Rachel glazed and stiff, and the tiny charcoal eyes fixed on him.

But Rachel and Sam slept on, and in time Jerra was left limp, with a clearmindedness that only came to him in this way.

In that dim room with its smells of talcum and incense and anchovy breath, he began to know his fear. To be a father. It frightened him. He had barely got the hang of being a son, and then Sam was born. He remembered how he and Rachel took him to the old man's bedside. No one failed to grasp the weight of that occasion when the baby smiled and quivered and the old man drank him up, his flesh, his scent, his life.

Cars rattled past on the street outside. The Bulgarian's dog was barking again. Nilsam pulled Sam to him. He slipped an arm under him and cupped the little buttocks in their pyjamas.

This morning he was lost. On that bicycle with his son, he was lost; there was a landmark gone. It was a year. The old man was dead. How could he be a father when he was lost? What could he navigate by? But hadn't he got by this past year?

Rachel turned with a sigh. He lifted the blind again. The faint light showed him her face. It was so familiar it might have been his own. He felt her breath on him. The house creaked. He knew where he was. The Bulgarian's dog barked. A Volkswagen pulled in next door. He even knew the time by that; it was four o'clock. A rooster crowed. His panic receded.

At dawn he took Sam in his arms out to the toilet. The grass was cold. Sam pissed on the seat. The homely, ammoniac smell made Nilsam grin. He hoisted the sleeping boy onto his shoulder and took him across the dewy lawn towards the house. Sun moved across the rooftops. A phrase of music came to him, something fresh which made his heart tick. This afternoon he would go and see his mother. Today he would do many things. He took the boy inside, put him in bed beside Rachel and climbed in. Sleep came to him and he was not afraid.

Barry Hill

HEADLOCKS

Late in the day the boy went to the front gate to look out for his father. Saturday: his father went down the road for a few drinks on Saturday, and he came home the long way; down the quarry road that gave a view of the sea two miles off, then down the hill towards the few blocks that were still paddocks. The boy met him at the same spot each week, and each week the father met the boy's expectations absolutely — listening to all that he had to say until they were indoors, were eating dinner, and drinking their tea quietly in the kitchen.

One afternoon the boy ran towards his father in the usual way, but found himself pulling up short: someone was with his father . . . When the boy wanted to withdraw like that, as he sometimes did when the man had a few too many drinks and was carelessly attentive, he thought of him as father rather than as the old man. But when things were good he was the old man, just as his father had called grandpa when he was still alive; a disrespectful term thought the relatives, though the boy knew, as his father always had, that it was not.

'Hi, Greg,' his father said. 'This is Mr Morrison, Ed Morrison.'

Greg said hello and the men went on walking.

Ed was about the same age as his father except he had more hair, with more oil on it. A tattoo covered the back of one hand while others seemed about to crawl out of his rolled-up shirt sleeves. As the men strolled along the footpath Greg walked slightly behind them, veering onto the nature strip whenever he tried to keep even. At the front gate he said to his father that the stumps were already in position in the backyard. But his father touched his shoulder and led Ed into the kitchen to meet his mother.

Once Ed had washed his hands and sat down at the table Greg brought out some of his drawings. 'Did you do all these yourself?' Ed said. 'That's good.'

The beer was poured. Greg put his collection of sinkers and hooks on the table, and Ed fiddled with the big hooks as he went on talking. Ed was telling his father about the mussels to be got from the docks at Alexandria, and his father was telling Ed that no one could have got better mussels than they had been getting from the local piers before the Italians came.

Greg went out into the backyard and came in with his lizards. He put the wooden seed box on the floor and lifted the cellophane. The smell of the dead ones wafted up towards the steaming corn beef that his mother had just placed on the table.

'He forgets to feed them,' his father informed Ed.

'I do not.' Greg looked up by way of appeal.

'No,' the old man added, 'we have trouble with our supply of fresh insects.'

'What you need to do is this,' said Ed, snatching the air. One by one Greg lifted the man's fingers until, wriggling in his palm, the fly appeared.

Mum had made the mayonnaise salad. Onto Ed's plate she piled an eggy oniony section, then Greg was allowed to help himself. It was a hot night; the back door was open, the dog was scratching near the step, and the crickets were going silly.

Ed and the old man were still talking. Mum looked on. Now and then Ed paused to pay her special attention, but at the end of the meal she insisted on clearing the table herself and carrying the dishes to the sink while the men went into the front room. Greg followed the men and sat on the floor near the window, beside the old man's chair. From where he was he could see ginger tufts of hair in his father's ear, and the face of Ed steadily flushing. A faint breeze came in through the venetian blinds.

The Middle East was mentioned again. Greg got up and left the room. He came back with an olive-green book that had as its first picture a painting of a troopship: on the deck dozens of wounded men sat about in the sun, or were stretched in the shade of lifeboats and tarpaulins. 'Yes,' said Ed excitedly, and Greg sat beside him while they thumbed through the pages. Presently, his mother came in waving a postcard.

Two men in shorts stood on a bare stretch of sand, hands behind their backs, grinning. No shirts, only their bare chests as brown or as dirty as their legs. The one with the slouch hat was Ed; the other was Uncle Allen, his mother's brother. 'Bet you haven't seen that for a while,' his mother said to Ed.

While Ed was looking, Greg tried to get as close to the card as possible. He almost scooped it out of Ed's hand.

'Looking at the bloody gun, are yuh,' said Ed. Hanging from his uncle's belt was a large revolver. 'Stand up a tick,' Ed said.

Taking up a position near the door, Ed told Greg to run towards him. 'Come on, just come at me,' he said, leaning forward with his arms loose, as if a dog was going to leap up at his face.

Greg took a few steps. In football the old man had taught him how to mock a run and spin off on the ball of the right foot. But here there was no room and before he got anywhere, Ed had turned him around and was holding the edge of the postcard at his throat. 'You don't really need a gun, see.'

'Now stand there,' Ed said, once he had let go.

Greg waited within inhaling distance of the man's breath. He knew the old man was watching so there was no need to turn around. Ed tightened the roll of his sleeves and fixed the buckle of his belt. 'Now I'll show you some of the crucial points. Your old man might have a bit to learn as well,' he said with a wink. Just then, Greg might well have turned, but Ed was already at work with his finger.

'Here,' he said, pressing a spot on Greg's neck, 'is where

they go out cold.' He grimaced as if he had pushed right in.

'Or, this way you don't have to worry about them either.' He pressed his knuckles into the boy's Adam's apple.

'Or here!' Swinging his arm up from the floor he brought his fist just short of the boy's groin. 'You might need to use some of these on the old man, one day. Never know.'

'He won't need to do anything of the sort,' Greg heard his mother say.

Ed laughed.

'I don't want anybody teaching him that sort of thing.' His mother smoked one cigarette a night and she had stubbed it out.

'I'm just giving the kid the science of the show. So he won't have to use guns.' Ed smiled and tapped his empty pockets.

'No, you're not. You're putting ideas into his head, crook ones,' his mother called.

Ed took a good look at the woman.

Greg had never seen his mother so pigheaded. She got like that when she rowed with his father. Now she sat stiff as a broomstick, while Ed shoved back the chairs.

Greg threw himself at the man's belly, butted the soft part so hard that Ed fell back with a grunt against the door. Greg dived at the floor and took hold of the man's knee, tried to bend it. Ed picked him up by the middle, turned him round and locked his wrists behind his back. Greg tried to kick his shins but they danced away.

'That's enough,' his mother snarled.

'One more, Mum.' He went limp until Ed let go.

'Now what you can't do,' Ed was saying, 'is run at someone like a Mallee bull. He'll have you down in no time, even if you're waving a knife.'

They started close, with Greg making a quick chop at the man's neck. A swipe at the other arm. Blocked again. Finally he lifted his knee — but collected a hip bone. 'Now stand back and we'll do it again,' Ed said.

Greg was flushed. He didn't speak — couldn't. Catch himself in the mirror, and he'd blubber for sure; catch the old man's eye, and he was done. He got ready to go at the enemy again . . .

'Stop it now, you're upsetting him.'

But Ed took no notice of his mother.

Oh, shut up, Mum, shut up, Greg thought, and then at last he heard: 'Let them go,' and it was the old man's voice and any minute he would . . . yes, *yes*.

This time, Greg thought, if Ed blocks my knee with his hip I'll be able to get my arm over as he bends. Then I'll have him in that headlock. When his face is down and his ears are jammed I'll get him onto the floor and before he can roll, straddle him. All I need to do is get my arm over quick enough . . . He went in with his eyes open. He saw Ed's face until the last instant, right up until they went down — down, it seemed, into the pile of the carpet.

The hot night pressed green and purple into the face and brown shot through his eyes so fast that he missed the first moves beside him. But together they pinned Ed down, one to each arm, then with the old man holding the shoulders, Greg bashed the man's skull against the floor. When the face was still he hit it a few times with the glass bottom of the ashtray.

They lifted together and carried the body outside where it went straight into a sugar bag; the old man tossed it over his shoulder and up the ladder they went to the roof of the garage where they'd piled newspapers and old boxes and wood. They watched the body burn until suddenly when the rocket went off, you didn't see it at all, not until it was coming down again, rekindling in the fall while he and the old man were laughing and yelling, hooting together like mad.

David Malouf

THE KYOGLE LINE

In July 1944, when train travel was still romantic, and hourly flights had not yet telescoped the distance between Brisbane and Sydney to a fifty-five-minute interval of air-conditioned vistas across a tumble of slow-motion foam, we set out, my parents, my sister and I, on the first trip of my life — that is how I thought of it — that would take me over a border. We left from Kyogle Station, just a hundred yards from where we lived, on a line that was foreign from the moment you embarked on it, since it ran only south out of the state and had a gauge of four-foot-eight. Our own Queensland lines were three-foot-six and started from Roma Street Station on the other side of the river.

I was familiar with all this business of gauges and lines from school, where our complicated railway system, and its origins in the jealously guarded sovereignty of our separate states, was part of our lessons and of local lore, but also because, for all the years of my later childhood, I had seen transports pass our house ferrying troops across the city from one station to the other, on their way to Townsville and the far north. We lived in a strip of no-man's-land between lines; or, so far as the thousands of Allied troops were concerned, between safe, cosmopolitan Sydney and the beginning, at Roma Street, of their passage to the war.

Our own journey was for a two weeks' stay at the Balfour Hotel at the corner of King and Elizabeth streets, Sydney. The owner was an old mate of my father's, which is why, in wartime, with all hotel rooms occupied, we had this rare chance of accommodation. Train bookings too were hard to come by. We would sit up for sixteen hours straight — maybe more, since the line was used for troop movements. I was delighted. It meant I could stay up all night. Staying awake past midnight was also, in its way, a border to be crossed.

I had been many times to see people off on the 'First Division', and loved the old-fashioned railway compartments with their foliated iron racks for luggage, their polished woodwork, the spotty black-and-white pictures of Nambucca Heads or the Warrumbungles, and the heavy brocade that covered the seats and was hooked in swags at the windows. When we arrived to claim our seats, people were already crammed into the corridor, some of them preparing to stand all the way. There were soldiers in winter uniform going on leave with long khaki packs, pairs of gum-chewing girls with bangles and pompadours, women with small kids already snotty or smelly with wet pants, serious men in felt hats and double-breasted suits. The afternoon as we left was dry and windy, but hot in the compartment. It was still officially winter. When the sun went down it would be cold.

My mother would spend the journey knitting. She was, at that time, engaged in making dressing-gowns, always of the same pattern and in the same mulberry-coloured nine-ply, for almost everyone she knew. There was rationing, but no coupons were needed for wool. I had been taught to knit at school and my mother let me do the belts — I had already made nine or ten of them — but was waiting because I didn't want to miss the border and the view.

What I was hungry for was some proof that the world was as varied as I wanted it to be; that somewhere, on the far side of what I knew, difference began, and that the point could be clearly recognised.

The view did change, and frequently, but not suddenly or sharply enough. It was a matter of geological forms I couldn't read, new variants of eucalypt and pine. The journey from this point of view was a failure, though I wouldn't admit it. I stayed excited and let my own vivid expectations colour the scene. Besides, it wasn't a fair test. We had barely passed the border when it was dark. It did get perceptibly colder. But was that a crossing into a new climate zone or just the ordinary change from day to night? The train rocked and sped, then jolted and stopped for interminable periods in a ringbarked nowhere; then jerked and clashed and started up again. We saw lights away in the darkness, isolated farmhouses or settlements suggesting that some of the space we were passing through was inhabited. We got grimy with smuts.

My mother knitted, even after the lights were lowered and other people had curled up under blankets. I too kept wide awake. I was afraid, as always, of missing something — the one thing that might happen or appear, that was the thing I was intended not to miss. If I did, a whole area of my life would be closed to me for ever.

So I was still awake, not long after midnight, when we pulled into Coffs Harbour and the train stopped to let people get off and walk for a bit, or buy tea at the refreshment room.

'Can *we*?' I pleaded. 'Wouldn't you like a nice cup of tea, Mummy? I could get it.'

My mother looked doubtful.

'It wouldn't do any harm,' my father said, 'to have a bit of a stretch.'

'I need to go to the lav,' I threw in, just to clinch the thing. It had been difficult to make your way through standing bodies and over sleeping ones to the cubicles at either end of the carriage. The last time we went we had to step over a couple, one of them a soldier, who were doing something under a blanket. My father, who was modest, had been shocked.

'Come on then.' We climbed down.

It was a clear cold night and felt excitingly different, fresher than I had ever known, with a clean smell of dark bushland sweeping away under stars to the escarpments of the Great Divide. People, some of them in dressing-gowns and carrying thermos flasks, were bustling along the platform. The train hissed and clanged. It was noisy; but the noise rose straight up into the starry night as if the air here were thinner, offered no resistance. It felt sharp in your lungs.

We passed a smoky waiting-room where soldiers were sprawled in their greatcoats, some on benches, others on the floor, their rifles in stacks against the wall; then the refreshment room with its crowded bar. It was a long walk to the Men's, all the length of the platform. I had never been out after midnight, and I expected it to be stranger. It *was* strange but not strange enough. In some ways the most different thing of all was to be taking a walk like this with my father.

We were shy of one another. He had always worked long hours, and like most children in those days I spent my time on the edge of my mother's world, always half-excluded but half-involved as well. My father's world was foreign to me. He disappeared into it at six o'clock, before my sister and I were up, and came back again at tea-time, not long before we were packed off to bed. If we went down under-the-house on Saturdays to watch him work, with a stub of indelible pencil behind his ear, as some men wear cigarettes, it was to enter a world of silence there that belonged to his deep communication with measurements, and tools, and dove-tail joints that cast us back on our own capacity for invention.

He was not much of a talker, our father. He seldom told us things unless we asked. Then he would answer our questions too carefully, as if he feared, with his own lack of schooling, that he might lead us wrong. And he never told stories, as our mother did, of his family and youth. His family were there to be seen, and however strange they might be in fact, did not lend themselves to fairytale. My father had gone out to work at twelve. If he never spoke of his youth it was, perhaps, because he had never had one, or because its joys and sorrows were of a kind we could not be expected to understand. There was no grand house to remember, as my mother remembered New Cross; no favourite maids; no vision of parents sweeping into the nursery to say goodnight in all the ballroom finery of leg-o'-mutton sleeves and pearl combs and shirt-fronts stiff as boards. His people were utterly ordinary. The fact that they were also *not* Australian, that they ate garlic and oil, smelled different, and spoke no English, was less important than that they had always been there and had to be taken as they were. Our father himself was as Australian as anyone could be — except for the name. He had made himself so. He had played football for the state, and was one of the toughest welterweights of his day, greatly admired for his fairness and skill by an entire generation.

But all this seemed accidental in him. A teetotaller and non-smoker, very quiet in manner, fastidiously modest, he had an inner life that was not declared. He had educated himself in the things that most interested him, but his way of going about them was his own; he had worked the rules out for himself. He suffered from never having been properly schooled, and must, I see now, have hidden deep hurts and humiliations under his studied calm. The best he could do with me was to make me elaborate playthings — box-kites, a three-foot yacht— and, for our backyard, a magnificent set of swings. My extravagance, high-strung fantasies, which my mother tended to encourage, intimidated him. He would have preferred me to become, as he had, a more conventional type. He felt excluded by my attachment to books.

So this walk together was in all ways unusual, not just because we were taking it at midnight in New South Wales.

We walked in silence, but with a strong sense, on my part at least, of our being together and at one. I liked my father. I wished he would talk to me and tell me things. I didn't know him. He puzzled me, as it puzzled me too that my mother, who was so down on our speaking or acting 'Australian', should be so fond of these things as they appeared, in their gentler form, in him. She had made, in his case, a unique dispensation.

On our way back from the Men's we found ourselves approaching a place where the crowd, which was generally very mobile, had stilled, forming a bunch round one of the goods wagons.

'What is it?' I wanted to know.

'What is it?' my father asked another fellow when we got close. We couldn't see anything.

'Nips,' the man told us. 'Bloody Nips. They got three Jap POWs in there.'

I expected my father to move away then, to move me on. If he does, I thought, I'll get lost. I wanted to see them.

But my father stood, and we worked our way into the centre of the crowd; and as people stepped away out of it we were drawn to the front, till we stood staring in through the door of a truck.

It was too big to be thought of as a cage, but was a cage, just the same. I thought of the circus wagons that sometimes came and camped in the little park beside South Brisbane Station, or on the waste ground under Grey Street Bridge.

There was no straw, no animal smell. The three Japs, in a group, if not actually chained then at least huddled, were difficult to make out in the half-dark. But looking in at them was like looking in from our own minds, our own lives, on another species. The vision imposed silence on the crowd. Only when they broke the spell by moving away did they mutter formulas, 'Bloody Japs,' or 'The bastards', that were meant to express what was inexpressible, the vast gap of darkness they felt existed here — a distance between people that had nothing to do with actual space, or the fact that you were breathing, out here in the still night of Australia, the same air. The experience was an isolating one. The moment you stepped out of the crowd and the shared sense of being part of it, you were alone.

My father felt it. As we walked away he was deeply silent. Our moment together was over. What was it that touched him? Was he thinking of a night, three years before, when the Commonwealth Police had arrested his father as an enemy alien?

My grandfather came to Brisbane from Lebanon in the 1880s; though in those days of course, when Australia was still unfederated, a parcel of rival states, Lebanon had no existence except in the mind of a few patriots. It was part of greater Syria; itself then a province of the great, sick Empire of the Turks. My grandfather had fled his homeland in the wake of a decade of massacres. Like other Lebanese Christians, he had sorrowfully turned his back on the Old Country and started life all over again in the New World.

His choice of Australia was an arbitrary one. No one knows why he made it. He might equally have gone to Boston or to Sao Paulo in Brazil. But the choice, once made, was binding. My father and the rest of us were Australians now. That was that. After Federation, in the purely notional view of these things that was practised by the immigration authorities, greater Syria (as opposed to Egypt and Turkey proper) was declared white — but only the Christian inhabitants of it, a set of official decisions, in the matter of boundary and distinction, that it was better not to question. My father's right to be an Australian, like any Scotsman's for example, was guaranteed by this purely notional view — that is, officially. The rest he had to establish for himself; most often with his fists. But my grandfather, by failing to get himself naturalised, remained an alien. At first a Syrian, later a Lebanese. And when Lebanon, as a dependency of France, declared for Vichy rather than the Free French, he became an enemy as well.

He was too old, at more than eighty, to be much concerned by any of this, and did not understand perhaps how a political decision made on the other side of the world had changed his status, after so long, on this one. He took the bag my aunts packed for him and went. It was my father who was, in his quiet way — what? shaken, angered, disillusioned?

The authorities — that is, the decent local representatives — soon recognised the absurdity of the thing and my grandfather was released: on personal grounds. My father never told us how he had managed it, or what happened, what he *felt,* when he went to fetch his father home. If it changed anything for him, the colour of his own history for example, he did not reveal it. It was just another of the things he kept to himself and buried. Like the language. He must, I understood later, have grown up speaking Arabic as well as he spoke Australian; his parents spoke little else. But I never heard him utter a word of it or give any indication that he understood. It went on as a whole layer of his experience, of his understanding and feeling for things, of alternative being, that could never be expressed. It too was part of the shyness between us.

We got my mother her nice cup of tea, and five minutes later, in a great bustle of latecomers and shouts and whistles, the train started up again and moved deeper into New South Wales. But I thought of it now as changed. Included in its string of lighted carriages, along with the sleeping soldiers and their packs and slouch-hats with sunbursts on the turn-up, the girls with their smeared lipstick and a wad of gum hardening now under a rim of the carriage-work, the kids blowing snotty bubbles, the men in business suits, was that darker wagon with the Japs.

Their presence imposed silence. That had been the first reaction. But what it provoked immediately after was some sort of inner argument or dialogue that was in a language I couldn't catch. It had the rhythm of the train wheels over those foreign four-foot-eight-inch rails — a different sound from the one our own trains made — and it went on even when the train stalled and waited, and long after we had come to Sydney and the end of our trip. It was, to me, as if I had all the time been on a different train from the one I thought. Which would take more than the sixteen hours the timetable announced and bring me at last to a different, unnameable destination.

Gerard Windsor

My Father's Version of the Nurses' Story

First the war, then medicine, came between my father and myself. In my first years and his most receptive years, my father had more things to do than hang around attending to me. He went to the war, he went to the Royal College of Surgeons. I stayed behind. He had chosen his ground, and I wasn't on it, then or ever.

So now, each from the safety of his own territory, my father and I circle round one another. We don't have much time and the questions are pressing. My father wants desperately to be proud of his children. I have reservations about his criteria, but I cannot resent the wish. He is becoming less certain about this writing business. He has always thought it an amateur affair — an after-hours activity anyone should be able to do. He has been writing all his life, he says, dozens and dozens of articles in medical journals. But now I hear him say, 'My son is a writer.' Old friends and colleagues tell him when they read something I write and find it marginally comprehensible. He offers no opinion himself. But he offers me subject matter. 'Come and see this operation,' he says. 'You might like to write about it.' He holds in his hand something I have written, and gestures with it. But he comments by way of something similar that happened to himself, or by recalling his presence at some event I have mentioned. He does not engage. Not that I demand he should. His feints are quite eloquent enough. He'll come closer in his own good time, I think. He has his own approach, his own style.

He comes at me obliquely. I approach him more directly. My strongest pull is to what is most foreign to me. There are possibilities there, I tell myself. I accept his invitation to go into the operating theatre. I check with him on medical details. I quiz him on symptoms and diagnoses and prognoses.

And I ask him about the war. I have not been to war. So I wonder and wonder about it. And I badger my father terribly about his war. I envy him. Tell me about a medical war, I ask him. Make something of it, I want to tell him. It must be a great clarifier. So my endeavours converge; I probe at the man, and I stick out my finger into the maelstrom.

I don't want any of the clichés, ancient or modern, about war. I know all that, I don't need a father for it. I keep prodding him on this event or that. I hope the individual will suddenly stand forth. But it's not easy going, getting the apocalyptic story out of him. He is ready to be dry, laconic. I prompt him with a photo album, and he does his tour of duty round the south-west Pacific. In the Ramu Valley he peers at thousands of glass plates, trying to identify the malaria bacillus in swabs taken from sick troops carried out of the jungle. He is warned not to be fooled by the fly shit. In Singapore he leads Lord Louis Mountbatten on a tour of his wards in the Fourteenth Australian General Hospital, and he says, 'I am just to the left outside the picture,' or 'I am standing just beside the photographer.' So he is not recorded with royalty.

I try to nudge him further towards the centre of things. 'Was most of the work with battle casualties?' I ask.

'No,' he says, 'mostly not.' And I think he is going to leave it at that. But he begins again. 'But the worst moment was . . . I suppose you could call it that . . . battle casualties. We were waiting in Moresby. The paratroopers had taken Nadzab. We were to fly there soon, but before we went more infantry had to follow up. They were waiting in a marshalling yard at the end of the runway. A Liberator, loaded with bombs and petrol, took off. It clipped a tree, staggered, and crashed beside a company of the waiting infantrymen. They were doused in burning petrol. We worked frantically. We cleaned the skin, removed the blisters, covered with vaseline gauze. We had rows of starkly red, shiny bodies. It was a terrible thing to do in the light of what we now know. They were literally flayed alive. Every one of them died.' My father is matter of fact. He can live with that. He has never had nightmares. Medicine has advanced. And medicine will never know very much. My father must have the perfect temperament for surgery. He has not a callous nerve in his body, but no amount of putrid or flayed or mashed flesh has ever dislocated him. All right, I say, a person can live with that. The images of the inferno are never likely to dull; they are not, God help us, uncommon. Nor even necessarily unsettling. They're on vicarious offer far too readily.

So I see no alternative but to move towards the most dangerous topic. The nurses' story is potentially his best one. But it's islanded amid reefs of sentimentality. And I refuse to be taken in by the merely sentimental. It's my father's besetting sin, sentimentality. I'm determined it won't be the final fruit we harvest from his war. But he's wary too, and I wonder if it's for the same reason. 'How did you come to be involved with the nurses?' I ask.

'Oh, it's in that book there,' he says, with as much amusement as pride, and he points to the shelf. 'You can read it all there.' It's Betty Jeffrey's *White Coolies*. He gets two mentions. It says he was there 'also'. And it says he told those POW nurses there was a ward ready. That's all. But there's more to it than that. The story absorbs me, and I can't believe it's meaningless to him. And I desperately hope that, for both of us, its strength is not as a tear-jerker. I hear it again on the radio, Tim Bowden's 'Just an Ordinary Bunch of Women', and I thank God I'm in a room by myself for I walk around trying to blink back the tears and biting my lip and barely able to restrain myself from sobbing. It's terrible. And I think, is there any way we can end that story, any way we can climax it without making the likes of the pair of us cry?

I don't want to let him build up the pathos of it. He'll give me the sinking of the *Vyner Brooke* and the machine-gunning of the survivors. So I prompt him, 'What was your part in it all at the end?'

'Oh, it was hardly more than a formality really,' he says. He seems unwilling to get started.

'Well, how did you get mixed up in it?' I try.

'I was just told to. Sam Langford, our commanding officer, told me there'd been reports of these nurses somewhere in Sumatra, and I was to locate them.' He is deliberately flat. It's not that he can't tell a story. He is simply dragging his feet, shying away from getting properly into motion.

'All the sisters attached to our C. C. S. had been among the lucky ones to escape from Singapore on the *Empire Star*. They spoke almost daily of their colleagues who had embarked on the *Vyner Brooke*. I knew so many of the names, I knew so many of the personalities. And now I was told to locate them.' My father thinks about that for a while, but doesn't say anything more about it. I'm glad. It's one of those points where the tears could well up very readily.

'We flew to Palembang. We circled twice over the runway, with its Zeros lined up on either side. The Japanese were courteous, wanted to know our business, offered us Kool cigarettes. They showed us to staff cars and drove the seven miles into the town. On the way other staff cars met us coming in the opposite direction. The officers in each case would signal to one another by twirling a sheathed sword through the window. The other car would join in behind us. We entered Palembang in a procession of ten staff cars. Japanese troops by the roadside stood at the salute.'

'It looks almost like a special disposition of providence,' I suggest.

A tremor, part puzzlement, part frown, moves across my father's face. I know he has no time for the intellectual gloss to his stories, but in his own way I think he'd agree with the point. I explain. 'I mean it was a very fitting detail that the nurses could have been liberated in such style.'

'I suppose so,' mutters my father, but without any

conviction, and as though he hasn't really heard me. I wonder myself whether it isn't a silly remark, and my father accepts it only because this is a pitfallen road he is travelling down, and he'll latch on to anything to prevent him slipping into one of his own emotional holes. Hell, I rebuke myself, it's not silly. It's one feature of the story that's as valid as any other. I could even argue that this wryly ironic climax forces itself on you.

'The nurses weren't in Palembang,' says my father, as though he's suddenly remembered why he takes exception to my gloss. 'We sent out our co-pilot in one of the staff cars, south-west, further into southern Sumatra. He found them, sent word to me, and got them to Lahat where there was a small airstrip. I immediately signalled Matron Sage. She was Matron-in-Chief. She had flown up from Australia and was waiting in Singapore for word of the girls she had inducted into the army.'

My father pauses. This is one of the danger moments. He can't help milking the emotion in the story. I want to hurry him on. But then I wonder whether I'm not just damming back the emotion for a spectacular finale, whether I'm not nervous that he's going to dissipate it bit by bit along the way. Beneath that, I think, I must be wondering whether he realises the potential and proper shape of his story. No, I say to both of us, it doesn't have to be a runaway tear-jerker. Let's just stick to the barest facts, and see what emerges.

'What did she do?' I ask.

'She decided to leave at once to meet them. She flew into Palembang and I was back there to meet her. She had a mishap which I'll always remember.'

I seize on this. 'Why? What happened?'

'As her plane landed it blew a tyre. It had to be taken off, repaired, blown-up again, and replaced. I had with me a chap by the name of Chisholm, a sergeant, and an ex-POW. We'd picked him up in Palembang, and I don't know whose, if anyone's, orders he was under. But he took charge of this repair job. He lined up twenty of the Japs and got them to work on the hand pump. As each one tired, Chisholm gave him a push on the arse with his boot, and the next in the queue took over.'

Well, well, I think, here's something to deflate the story.

My father is chuckling. It seems rather distasteful to me. I would like it to be a large comic moment, but it refuses to slip into that shape. The picture I see is of Australian jackboots blasting, in a great shower of sparks and stars, wizened, malevolent, pear-shaped Japanese pygmies all over the sky. Stock figures, a stock picture. No, that won't fit in with the dignity of this saga. But then maybe that's all the story needs to save it from the gross sentimentality of the likes of my father and myself. The tears will get dried out pretty quickly once there's this constant flicker of anthropoid little men lining up, bending over, and being punted, tapped and drop-kicked all over the field.

'He was remarkably gentle,' says my father. 'I don't know what sort of life he'd had as a POW, but this way of getting his own back was heckuva mild. He was a bit of an actor, Chisholm. Being nasty to the Japs didn't seem to be in his mind at all. He only had the one old hand pump, and he just used the most efficient method he could. Nobody got hurt or worked too hard; that would have defeated the purpose of it. He just liked the experience once again, at long last, of being in charge and able to give orders. Getting his dignity back. So he posed and strutted a bit, and generally over-acted the part. But with a healthy twinkle in his eye the whole time.' My father chuckles, remembering Chisholm.

If my father insists that's the way it was, I don't see how I can make anything else out of it. I don't see how I can stop the acceleration at this point. My father seems quite happy now to go on. 'We took off as soon as the tyre had been fixed. The flight took twenty-five minutes. As the plane landed we could see a group of people sitting under an awning on the edge of the strip.'

That's good. He's very matter of fact.

'They didn't stand up. They didn't wave. There weren't very many of them. It wasn't one of those delirious, crowd-scene arrivals at all. They waited. We taxied through the long grass. We could hear it hissing against the undercarriage and over the roar of the engines and the rumble of the wheels. We wobbled to a halt. The co-pilot pushed open the door, and the ladder went down. I stepped out.'

'You stepped out first?'

'Yes.'

'Why did you step out first?'

'Heavens, boy, it was instinctive.'

'Yes, but why?'

'Because that's what you do in those sorts of circumstances. I wasn't just going through any old sort of door. Damn it all, if it's dangerous or difficult or a man can be of some use, he goes first. Doesn't he?' My father brushes aside the triviality of it.

'Yes, I suppose so.' I give up trying to direct him.

'Matron Sage got out. I stood back. I thought she should go first. And she walked . . .'

My father stood back. He thought Matron Sage should go first. I am seized by the off-hand detail. But any man of any sensitivity would have done that, I tell myself. Oh yes! I am answered. Look at the pressures he resisted without any forethought, any tensing himself. So I look at them. He is keyed up. He is first off the plane and has a head start. He is the senior man. He has been in charge of locating and rescuing these women. He has now arrived to liberate them. He knows all the details of what to tell them, of what arrangements have been made for them. He is a doctor and they are nurses. He is a man and his instincts must prompt him to play the gallant deliverer. And he is a young man and these are young women. But my father stands back.

And Matron Sage walks towards her girls. They are wraiths, they are like the spirits in prison that Christ visited. And now at last they rise up. And the long grass opens and Matron Sage moves towards them, her daughters, and you can hear the sobs bursting through her outstretched arms. She stands there in her felt hat and her grey jacket and grey trousers and takes each of her daughters to her breast. And she asks the echoing question of those months, 'And where are the others?' and of course they give the echoing answer, 'This is all of us, Matron'. And Matron Sage and the girls stare at the incomprehensible horror and joy of it all.

And my father stands back, and tries to stand further back, but he cannot. He is forced to watch and hear everything, and he cannot get away to any other spot. He is forced to hear these words and see these faces. He does not want these tears, but he cannot escape them. They have staked out this plot. It belongs to them alone. And willy-nilly I am tied to him and caught also. It's no good, no good at all. My father and I sit there and cry away together. Other people falter on the edge of the room, and go away again.

Olga Masters

THE CHRISTMAS PARCEL

Christmas in 1935 would have been a dreary affair for the Churchers but for a parcel, more like a small crate, sent from the eldest, Maxine, in Sydney.

Maxine was eighteen, and had been away two years. The first Christmas she sent a card, and the Churchers were delighted with this and stood it against the milk jug on the table for Christmas dinner, which was baked stuffed rabbit, for they were plentiful, but money was not.

The next Christmas Eve the driver of the mail car gave several long blasts on the horn passing the paddocks where the Churcher children were standing, spindly legged among the saplings and tussocks, trying to invent a game to ward off disappointment that there would be no presents.

Their mother had warned them. Sometimes she cried softly as she told them, sometimes she was angry and blamed their father for his inability to find work, sometimes she was optimistic, indulging in a spasm of house cleaning, washing curtains and bedclothes, whitewashing the fireplace ready to fill with gum tips, and scrubbing the floorboards until they came up a grey white, like sand on some untouched beach.

Who knows, something might turn up, she would say as she worked. Her better-off sisters in distant towns might send a ten-shilling note in their Christmas cards, which would buy lollies, cordial, oranges, bananas, and raisins for a pudding, and be damned to Fred Rossmore who would expect it paid off the account, owing now for half a year.

The clean house gave her spirits a lift, as if they were cleansed too, and she would finish off the day by bathing all the children in a tub in front of the stove, adding a kettle of hot water with each one, washing their heads as well, and sending them out to sit on the edge of the veranda and share a towel, very threadbare, to dry.

Their old skimpy shirts and dresses were usually not fastened properly; it didn't matter, it would be bedtime soon.

The young Churchers would feel lighter in spirit too, sniffing at the soap lingering on them, although it was the same Mrs Churcher used to wash the clothes. They would look forward to fried scones for tea, and some stewed peaches, a small greenish variety, sour near the stone, eaten bravely while trying to avoid thinking of the sugar and cream that would make them so much more palatable.

Mr and Mrs Churcher were sitting on the woodheap when the mail car driver blew the horn through a cloud of dust.

'And a Merry Christmas to you too!' Mrs Churcher shouted. She was in a black mood, and Mr Churcher feared it and feared for the children, soon to trail home, not giving in readily to the futility of hanging stockings. While she angrily shuffled a foot among the chips, he looked at the children like stringy saplings themselves, some like small scarecrows, for they were playing a game with arms outstretched, their ragged old shapeless clothes flapping in the wind that had sprung up, kindly cooling the air after one of the hottest days of the summer.

Mr Churcher watched as one of them suddenly tore off to the track that led to the road. It was Lionel, racing hard and soon lost to sight where the track disappeared into a patch of myrtle bush. Mr Churcher was surprised at the energy with which Lionel ran. He worried about the children not getting enough to eat, but perhaps they were doing better than he thought. Anyone who could run like that after tearing about all day must be suitably fuelled. He felt a little happier, and looked at Mrs Churcher, surprised she was not sharing this feeling. She looked over the top of their grey slab house at some puffed up clouds, but not seeing them, he was sure, for the clouds had a milky transparency and he foolishly thought they would have a softening effect upon her. But her face wore a cloud of another kind, dark and thunderous. There was mutiny in her dark eyes, creased narrowly, not wide and soft, not even her body was soft, but gone tight in the old marocain dress, practically the only one she owned.

'I'll chop the head off the wyandotte,' Mr Churcher said. He was proud of his knowledge of poultry, and they had a cross breeding in their meagre fowl-run, comprising castoffs from other, fussier, farmers who pitied the impoverished state of the Churchers.

They rented their old place from the Heffernans, who had built it as their first home when they settled on the land fifty years earlier. Heffernan bought an adjoining property as fortunes improved and used the old place to run cattle. Since the house wasn't fenced in it was difficult, due to wandering steers, to grow produce to feed the eight children, or seven, now that Maxine had gone.

Mr Churcher was in constant conflict with Jim Heffernan. He (Mr Churcher) considered the five shillings a week rent unreasonable; he was actually doing the Heffernans a favour living there in a caretaking capacity, stopping the house from falling into ruin. He never tired of pointing out the work he put into the fowl-run, although he had actually stolen some wire netting from a bundle delivered to the roadside for the Heffernans to extend their kitchen garden. Mr Churcher saw the heap and sent Lionel for pliers to snip a length from a roll, which he was sure would escape the notice of the Heffernans.

Mrs Churcher was distressed to see the children a witness to theft, but put those feelings to one side when she saw Mr Churcher had made a good job of the pen and more eggs appeared, since the fowls did not continue to lay in obscure places like inside blackberry bushes and up hollow logs.

Mr Churcher was thinking now of making some reference to the fowl-pen to expose (once again) a more commendable side of his character and get him into his wife's good graces, although he did not think there was much chance of this. He took up the axe and spat on the blade, rubbing the spittle along the edge.

'I'll chop off its head before they get here,' he said, seeing the ragged little army, still several hundred yards off.

'It'll be tough as an old boot,' Mrs Churcher said looking at his. Her own feet were bare.

'It'll make good gravy and there's plenty of 'taters,' he said, injecting cheer into his voice.

Mrs Churcher was going to say the dripping to roast the fowl in was needed for their bread, for they had not eaten butter in weeks, when a shrill cry made her look towards the myrtle patch on the rise.

Lionel came screaming out of it, like a brown leaf bowling along, aided by a strong wind, his feet beating so hard upon the earth, Mr and Mrs Churcher expected the vibrations to be felt at the woodheap. They stood up.

'He's bitten! A snake's got him!' she cried out. (Her mood would not allow for anything but the worst news.)

But Lionel had stopped yelling to fly towards the woodheap, with the other children breaking into a run and shouting wildly too.

Lionel flung himself upon his father. He was a skinny boy of eight, so red of face now his freckles had disappeared in what looked like a wash of scarlet sweat. His brown straight hair, in need of a cut, was standing upright in spikes or plastered to his wet ears. His chest, no bigger it seemed than a golden syrup can, heaved and thudded and his little stick-like arms were trembling.

'It's a parcel! The biggest I've even seen! With Dad's name on it! Mr Barney Churcher, it says. And there's a million stamps!'

That was as much as he could say. He breathed and puffed and held his father's waist for support.

'Barney Churcher! That's me!' Mr Churcher said. He stroked down his front and looked up the track. 'That's me all right!'

Lionel sat panting on a block of wood. 'Oh, it's big, it's so big!'

The other children, all six of them, had reached the

woodheap by this time. Ernestine was first. She was thirteen, and fairly fleet of foot too. 'The mail car left us a parcel!' she called back to the running knot.

'Big!' Lionel cried now, with enough breath back to stand and throw his arms wide. 'Take the slide for it!'

'Hear that boy!' said Mr Churcher looking at Mrs Churcher, watching for the film of ugliness to slide from her face. He's a smart boy and he's ours, was the pleading message in his eyes.

'Go and get whatever it is, and I'll stoke the stove, for God knows what we'll eat,' Mrs Churcher said, walking off. Mr Churcher told himself her body was softening up a little and that was something.

'Come on!' he called, sounding no older than Lionel, and seizing the rope attached to the slide standing on its end by the tank-stand. The slide flew wide with the great tug Mr Churcher gave it, and the children laughed as they jumped out of its way.

'Lionel should get a ride!' Ernestine cried. She was brown haired and slender like Maxine, and would be a beauty too.

'He should and will!' Mr Churcher shouted and steadied the slide while Lionel climbed on and made a small heap of himself in the middle. Raymond, who was fifteen, took a part of the rope, and like two eager horses with heads down, father and son raced ahead, the slide flying over the brittle grass, barely easing its pace up the rise.

The parcel was from Maxine. They knew her writing. The contents were enclosed in several sheets of brown paper, then the lot wedged into a frame of well-spaced slats. Mr Churcher's name and their address was written on a label nailed to one side. Above the writing was a line of stamps, some heavily smudged with the stamp of the post office through which it was sent.

Mr Churcher and the children crowded around it, sitting by the sliprails, the gate long gone, unhinged by the Heffernans and used on their new property. All of them, even four-year-old Clifford who had ridden to the road on Ernestine's back, bent over the parcel, stroking the paper, patting the wood, jumping back to keep their eyes on it, as if it might disappear. How different the road, the sliprails, the deeply rutted track leading to the house, looked with it there. Leave it, leave it! cried part of the minds of the Churchers. Take it away and the emptiness will be more than we can bear!

'Come on!' called Mr Churcher, as if he too had to discipline himself to break the spell. He flung the parcel onto the slide and put Clifford beside it.

'Not too fast!' cried six-year-old Josephine, who was not as sturdy as the others and suffered bronchitis every winter. Ernestine took her on her back for she was no heavier than Clifford. She whispered into Ernestine's neck that the parcel might be opened before everyone was there, for Mr Churcher and Raymond were flying down the track with the wind taking all of Clifford's hair backwards.

'No, no!' cried Ernestine, breaking into an energetic jog. 'We'll all be there!'

Mrs Churcher was watching the track. 'There's Mum!' Clifford shouted.

'We got it!' screamed Lawrence, who was nine and between Gloria and Lionel in age. (Which accounts for all the Churcher children.)

Mrs Churcher watched, as if mesmerised, the parcel sliding to a stop at the edge of the veranda. Mr Churcher took his eyes off it to fasten them on her face. A crease at each corner of her mouth kept any threatened softness at a distance.

'From Maxine,' Mr Churcher said, pleading. He looked down on it beside Clifford, who was still on the slide reluctant to climb off.

'The stamps,' Mr Churcher said, touching them with his boot. 'Look what it cost even to send it.'

'It's a parcel for us for Christmas, Mum!' Ernestine said, brown eyes like her mother's begging with some impatience for her excitement.

'There'll be nothing to eat in it,' Mrs Churcher said. 'Toys and rubbish, I'll bet.' She looked hard at it, perhaps to avoid the eyes of the children, every pair on her she felt.

'I'll knock the old chook's head off!' Mr Churcher said.

'Not Wynie!' came in a chorus from most of them.

Gloria, who had wild red hair, sat on the edge of the veranda and held her bare feet. 'We can eat anything,' she murmured dreamily.

'Anything you'll be eating too!' Mrs Churcher said.

'It's soft,' Lionel said. 'So I reckon it's clothes. Clothes.' The light in his eyes ran like a small and gentle fire setting alight the eyes of the others.

'It's heavy, even for Dad,' Ernestine said. 'There's something in there for you, Mum, I reckon. New plates, like you want.'

'Plates! They'd smash to smithereens. We'll be sticking with the tin ones!' Her eyes rested briefly on Mr Churcher. It's your fault they're only tin, they said.

Mr Churcher looked down on his hands wishing for a cigarette to use them, but he had no tobacco. There might be tobacco in the parcel. Yes! A packet of Log Cabin and papers. Two packets. Maxine used to sit on his knee and watch him roll cigarettes when she was a little thing, no more than two and the only one. They thought there would be no more and life would be fairly easy with the Great War finished and not too many joined up from Cobargo, thank heavens, to show him up. (He had no sense of adventure where war was concerned, no inclination to join in the fighting.)

They had rented a little place in the town for six shillings a week (one shilling more than this and a palace in comparison, as he was always threatening to inform Jim Heffernan) and he had work, stripping bark, cutting eucalyptus, navvying on the road now and again. But the Depression came, and so did the children. Sometimes he went away for work, down as far as Moruya, coming home with his clothes in one sugar bag and some produce in another, oysters one time which the children had never tasted and passionfruit, which had been growing wild on the side of a mountain cleared for a new road. Mrs Churcher waited hopefully for him to produce some money, but there was always little of this. Once there was a pound note which the children looked upon as a fortune. It was a terrible disappointment to them when Mrs Churcher gave it to Fred Rossmore to ensure credit for a few more weeks.

Mr Churcher was thinking of past homecomings now, looking at the parcel, still on the slide with Clifford, irrelevant thoughts, for they concerned Maxine, not likely to come home herself, spending all that money on things for them. The children saw. They found other things to look at momentarily, but in a while their glances strayed back.

'Did any of you find any eggs today?' Mrs Churcher said. (For the fowls had found means of escaping the pen and were reverting to former laying habits.) They had not, it seemed. They stared at the parcel, as if the remark had insulted it.

'Then what do we eat?' Mrs Churcher said. She did not look at Mr Churcher, who turned his face towards the paddocks, hard and dry like his throat.

'You'll find something, Mum,' Ernestine said. 'You always do.'

'There comes a time when you don't!' Mrs Churcher said. 'It's come at Christmas. A good time to arrive!'

Her voice, hard as the baked, brittle paddocks, gave the words a ringing sound like an iron bar striking earth it couldn't penetrate.

Mr Churcher longed for an early evening, for long striped shadows to bring a softness to the hard, harsh day.

'Will we have nothing for Christmas dinner?' Clifford said, huddled and dreamy on the slide. The others felt their bodies twitch, hungrier suddenly than they were before.

'Remember last year?' Gloria said. 'We had baked rabbit and Maxie's card.'

'This year is better,' Lionel said. 'We got the parcel.'

'If Mum will let us open it,' Gloria said.

Mr Churcher looked at Mrs Churcher's set face.

'It's not addressed to me,' she said.

Mr Churcher slapped a top pocket as if tobacco were already there. 'It's not Christmas yet,' he said. They looked at the setting sun filling the sky with salmon and peach jam and beaten egg white.

'We'll go into town and ask Fred Rossmore for some stuff!' Now he was patting his pockets as if money were there. He put his hands down and his face away. 'We can pay after Christmas.'

'With the endowment money I want something for the kids to wear back to school!' Mrs Churcher cried.

The children wondered briefly which of them might have got something new.

'There might be things in here we could wear,' Lionel said, with a gentle toe on the brown paper.

'Come on!' Mr Churcher said, and began to walk rapidly off. He was taking the short cut through the bush, cutting off a quarter of a mile of road. Lionel ran to him and they both stopped and looked back to see who else was coming. Even with distance Mr Churcher's face showed he wanted Ernestine.

'I'll get my shoes and carry them!' she said, and was in and out of the room where the girls slept before Mr Churcher turned his head towards the track again. She ran to her father, not looking back.

Raymond, after standing with legs apart for a moment, holding his braces with fingers hooked in them, let the braces snap back into place and followed, racing past the little group to sit on a log some hundred yards ahead and wait, picking up bits of dead wood, rabbit dung and anything big enough to throw at nothing.

After a while they were lost to sight of those on the veranda, the gums and wattles and grey white logs, their roots exposed like a mouthful of rotten teeth, swallowing them up.

'I wonder what they'll bring back?' murmured Gloria. Clifford stood up and jumped off the slide, a very small jump he tried to make big. Lawrence moved along from his place on the veranda and put both feet on the slide.

'I'll stay with the parcel and mind it,' he said.

Mrs Churcher padded to the kitchen, opening the stove door and shutting it with a clatter of metal so loud Gloria came uneasily inside.

'Did you see that?' Mrs Churcher said, sitting with her knees spread, stretching the marocain until you saw through it.

Gloria did not know what she should have seen.

'Him!' Mrs Churcher said.

That meant Mr Churcher. That much she did know.

'Do you know why he made Ernestine go?'

No, Gloria didn't. Her chest went tight. Perhaps Ernie was his favourite. She (Gloria) was ugly (she thought). She and Lawrence were the two heavily freckled and with bright red hair. She had only sandshoes and could not have gone to town on Christmas Eve. Not that she would cry about it. There might be shoes in the parcel for her. She sat forward in her chair so that she saw a corner of it, watched by Lawrence, Josephine and Clifford, close together on the veranda edge. She was sorry she had come inside. Her mother strode to the stove now and put in a piece of wood Gloria thought too big and green to burn properly.

When Mrs Churcher went back to sit by the kitchen table she put her head on her arm and began to cry. 'Rotten men!' she said, sitting up suddenly and wiping her eyes with her fingers.

A thin smoke began to bathe the log in the stove and some of it ran out of the stove door. 'You need some chips,' Gloria said, anxious that her father should not be blamed too harshly for the wood he had brought in. Perhaps it was the smoke that sent more tears running down Mrs Churcher's cheeks.

'He took her with him to get stuff easier from Fred Rossmore!' Mrs Churcher said. 'I know Fred Rossmore!'

Of course, Gloria thought. Everyone in Cobargo did. Even children knew he was a powerful man in the town.

'He's fond of girls,' Mrs Churcher said. That seemed all right in Gloria's view, except for the tone of her mother's voice (like an iron bar on hard dry earth it couldn't penetrate).

'Huh!' Mrs Churcher said, which could be interpreted as

meaning that Gloria knew precious little about Fred Rossmore's character. 'Not for their good, but for his!' Mrs Churcher said.

Gloria pondered this. It appeared to mean that with Ernestine there, Fred Rossmore would not be handing out goods from his shelves. Her heart was troubled for her father coming in empty handed.

'He touches diddies if you let him,' Mrs Churcher said. 'And up here.' She touched the marocain stretched across her chest.

Gloria considered this a small price for butter, bacon, tinned peaches and biscuits, but dared not say so.

'And that parcel,' Mrs Churcher said. 'I wonder about that.'

Gloria bent forward again to see it, the most innocent thing in all the world.

'To start with, a man would put it in a frame like that. Not her.'

I wish she wouldn't say her, Gloria thought. Maxine had the nicest name of them all. Ernestine was next. After that it seemed Mrs Churcher's selection of names was clouded by her worries at feeding and clothing them all. Gloria had been told an aunt, a sister of her father, had named her after the film star Gloria Swanson. Gloria felt a deep shame that she failed to turn out looking anything like Miss Swanson.

The green wood was filling the kitchen with smoke and Mrs Churcher got up and rubbed it into the hot ashes for it to burn quicker.

'For all we know a man might have bought what's in it. I reckon he did.'

'For touching her diddie?' Gloria said.

Mrs Churcher was across the room in a second with a slap across Gloria's face so violent, Gloria lost her balance on the chair, and the noise brought the three from the veranda running to the door. They returned almost at once.

'Only Mum whacking Gloria,' Clifford said, sitting down even closer to the parcel.

'There!' Mrs Churcher said, working the legs of the

chair into the floor as she sat down. Gloria lay her face on her knee and cried softly. Mrs Churcher also cried. She allowed the tears to run in a great hurry down her cheeks, and when Gloria lifted her head she was surprised to see her mother's eyes quite bright and her face quite soft. She left her chair and went and sat on her knee. The fold of her stomach was soft as a mattress, and her shoulder a pillow, a fragrant fleshy pillow.

Mrs Churcher began to rock Gloria and this appeared to set them both crying without sound. When the others came in, tired of waiting by the parcel, Gloria lowered her face and Mrs Churcher turned hers. But they saw enough to make their eyes water too, so they moved together in a little bunch and stood giving all their attention to the stove fire.

Lawrence went off and returned with his old hat full of peaches. Gloria brought in some spindly wood that helped the green piece burn. Josephine asked if she could set the table, and Gloria, frowning on her, said to bring in some clothes from the line. The peaches were not as small and hard as those usually found, and when they had rolled to a stop on the table and Gloria brought a saucepan and a knife, Mrs Churcher said: 'You'd better let me.'

The four of them pressed their small chests against the edge of the table as they watched the peeling. It was a miracle of thinness, the furry skin falling from the knife like pale green tissue paper. Look at our Mum, said their eyes to each other. If only there was sugar to shake on some spoonfuls, without spilling a grain.

Mr Churcher brought some. Clifford, going out to check on the parcel, saw them come out of the bush and start their troop across to the house. He yelled as loud as Lionel when he found the parcel.

'They've got something!' he cried, flying inside then out again. The others followed except Mrs Churcher, who went to the stove with the saucepan of peaches and stayed there, making sure the lid was tight and they were on the right part of the stove to cook gently. Gloria allowed herself a brief look at the returning party, then when her mother had hung up the hessian oven rag, she went and hooped both arms around her and lay her face in the hollow of her breasts.

'They're coming,' Mrs Churcher said, not actually pushing her off.

'Sugar, Mum!' Lawrence cried, as Mr Churcher put the little brown bag on the table with two tins of herrings in tomato sauce, some cheese, cut into such a beautiful triangle it would be a shame to disturb it, and a half pound packet of tea and some dried peas.

'And look what Ernie's got!' Lionel cried, stepping aside from in front of her to reveal her holding clasped against her waist a paper bag. Everyone knew, by the little squares and rolls and balls making little bulges in the paper, it could be nothing else but sweets.

'Lollies!' screamed Clifford, and Mrs Churcher turned to the stove again and they saw by the neck showing under the thick straggling bun of her grey and black hair that she was crying.

'Stop crying, Mum,' Joseph said. 'Ernie will give you one.'

'They're for all of us to share,' Raymond said, in case anyone should begin to think differently. He sat on the door-step with a glance backwards at the parcel, the afternoon sun making diamonds of the tacks holding the label in place.

'Mum's not well,' Mr Churcher said. He was standing in the middle of the room, one hand near his waist, the fingers spread as if a cigarette was there. 'She's having another one.'

Mrs Churcher sat and found the hem of her petticoat to wipe her nose.

'It'll be the last,' Mr Churcher said.

The eyes of the children said this might or might not be so. Ernestine put the bag of sweets at the end of the top shelf of the dresser and snapped the glass doors shut. She moved to the table and put the other things from Fred Rossmore's inside the food safe. Mrs Churcher's wet eyes followed her. Ernestine's old sleeveless print dress showed her round tanned arms, and her hair heavy as a bird's nest showed bits of her neck, pure white inside dark brown slits. She brought out flour to make fried scones, holding the bag between breasts beginning to pout. Tears ran over Mrs Churcher's cheeks as Ernestine lowered the flour to the table and took a mixing bowl from a crude shelf above her head.

'There's four boys and four girls in this family,' Lionel said. 'So the next one can be anything it likes.'

Mr Churcher was on a chair with his elbows on his knees. 'Well said, Lionel. A smart boy that.' He longed to be brave enough to look into Mrs Churcher's eyes. 'You're all smart, all of you,' he said.

Raymond looked at the kitchen floorboards between his feet. He had left school a year ago, and still had no job except for trapping rabbits in the winter and selling the skins, a great pile of them for only five shillings. The tips of his ears were very red.

'Next year things are going to be better,' Mr Churcher said. Everyone half believed it, and Mrs Churcher, as if her mind were on something else, took out the sugar, and carrying it to the stove tipped a little onto the peaches. They all watched her fold the top of the bag down letting nothing escape.

'Yes, I reckon next year will be better,' Mr Churcher said, putting a hand to a back pocket and moving it around there, as if making room for a packet of tobacco.

'And there's the parcel!' he said, throwing back his head suddenly like a terrier about to bark.

Josephine flung herself on Ernestine, as if the excitement was too much to bear alone. Raymond drew himself into a tight ball with his face crushed between his knees.

Lionel and Lawrence went to the veranda to each put a light foot on the parcel. Clifford climbed onto his father's knee, and Gloria leaned against her mother, with the cheek still red from the slap rubbing gently into her marocain shoulder.

'And it's Christmas tomorrow!' Mr Churcher said, with his head back again and the words coming out like a terrier's bark. Out of the corner of his eye he saw Mrs Churcher's face start to go soft, then tighten again. She stood, taller than normal, he thought, and looked across at him. Her eyes swept the children to one side. She might have sent them from the room, though all were there, faces tipped up at her, eyes begging for harmony.

'That parcel was sent from the place where the bad girls are,' she said.

There was a rush for the veranda to look at the parcel again. Even Mr Churcher screwed his head towards it, but turned it back almost at once. His face did not believe it.

Gloria had a vision of a great mass of girls with pinched and sorrowful faces and their skirts dented deeply in the region of their diddies. She looked at Ernestine, who was measuring flour into a bowl with lowered eyes, but there was nothing to be seen past her waist, which was level with the table.

'Make sure you sift that flour properly,' Mrs Churcher said. Then she sat on a chair with her head up, not looking at Mr Churcher. 'You can see on the stamps where it was sent from.'

'She could have given it to anyone to post. It's a great thing to lug herself,' Mr Churcher said.

'She never writes,' Mrs Churcher said.

'She was saving up for all those stamps,' Mr Churcher answered. He got up and went and pulled the label from the parcel, looking at the stamps and postmark.

'You see it? Kings Cross! That's where she is!' Mrs Churcher took the bowl of flour from Ernestine and buried her hands in it. She began to cry again.

Mr Churcher put the label in the dresser next to the lollies from Fred Rossmore.

'Now it doesn't matter where it came from,' Lionel said. Mr Churcher's eyes told Lionel this was wisely said.

Josephine went to Ernestine to cry into her waist. 'We'll never know what's in the parcel!' she wailed.

'That's right!' Mrs Churcher was mixing dough fast with a knife, her tears temporarily halted. 'We'll send it back!'

Josephine wept louder and Ernestine, checking that her mother's hands were covered with dough, and Josephine seemed safe from a blow, held her very tight.

Raymond went pale, and the freckles stood out on Gloria and Lawrence for their faces had a pallor too. Lionel, sitting suddenly beside Raymond, turned the sole of one foot up and looked long and intently on it.

'You're a cruel woman, Maudie,' Mr Churcher said.

The children were not as frightened by his words as they might have been. He called Mrs Churcher Maudie in the soft moments.

Mrs Churcher, her face clear of tears, tossed her head high and banged the frying pan on the stove. It was not a terribly loud bang though.

'I know my Maxie,' Mr Churcher said. He was seated with his elbows on his knees. He held two fingers near his face and the children looked hard to be sure he had no cigarette.

'Your Maxie!' Mrs Churcher said.

'Our Maxie!' Mr Churcher said. 'A good girl!'

'Yes, yes, yes!' came in different voices, Josephine's the strangest, for she was laughing as well as sobbing. Ernestine wandered outside, still holding Josephine, and Gloria followed.

Under the old apricot tree, from which the fruit had been early and hungrily stripped, they put their backs to the trunk.

'I'm frightened,' Gloria said. 'If there are gold and jewels in that parcel, what will we do?'

Ernestine tried to shrink the parcel in her vision. Mr Churcher came to the back door and filled the opening. Ernestine, Gloria and Josephine went and sat at his feet on the slabs laid on the earth to make a rough veranda.

Ernestine bound her body in her arms and rocked herself a little while, looking away to the mountains gone black to show the sunset up all the brighter.

She lifted her face, no less lovely, to her father. 'You open the parcel, Dad. Like Mum said, it's addressed to you.'

'By jove I think I might!' Mr Churcher said, loud enough to swing Mrs Churcher's face from the food safe to which she was returning the flour.

'I'm setting the table here,' Mrs Churcher said. 'Without any help as usual!'

'Leave the table setting!' Mr Churcher said. 'I'm bringing in the parcel!'

He didn't go through the kitchen but strode around the house with Ernestine, Gloria and Josephine clinging to him.

Raymond, Lawrence, Lionel and Clifford were around the slide when they reached it. Mr Churcher lifted the parcel as if it were a pillow.

'Our Dad's so strong!' cried Lawrence. They stepped back like a guard of honour for him to go to the kitchen. He laid it on the table end.

'Don't break the box!' Lionel said. 'It'll be handy for something!'

'A doll's cradle!' Gloria said. 'If there's a doll in there for Josie!' Her eyes then sent an agonised apology to her mother.

There was no doll in there. But Josephine forgot her disappointment when the paper was pulled away and Ernestine held up a quilt, a snowy white fringed quilt with the honeycomb pattern broken up with a design of roses as big as cabbages, and trailing stems and leaves.

'Look at that!' someone cried.

'For Mum's bed!'

'And Dad's!'

Ernestine put it tenderly on a chair.

'Towels!' shrieked Gloria as four were found inside and four sheets with only a little fraying at the hems.

After that came a tablecloth, heavy and white, a beautiful thing for Christmas dinner, and several tea towels.

Ernestine held them up against the open doorway and there was hardly any wear showing.

'Give them all to Mum!' Gloria cried.

Mrs Churcher was on a chair, hands on her thighs, trying to keep the hardness in her eyes.

Mr Churcher sat on the doorstep where Raymond had been. He was watching Ernestine, Gloria and Lionel come to the end of the parcel.

Lionel shrieked when he held up a single page with Maxine's writing on it.

'I hope you like these things,' she wrote. 'I work for these people called Pattens. Mr Patten has a shop. He brought home some new sheets and things, all in colours which is the new fashion now. Mrs Patten decided to give me the old ones, or some of them, to send to you. She is not paying me this week, but says she has a Christmas present for me. They are having roast pork for Christmas dinner here, but I would rather be having what you are.'

Lionel read the letter and everyone hearing it was quiet.

Mrs Churcher bent down to look into the stove fire, which was smoking again, so she needed to find her petticoat hem to wipe her eyes and nose.

Mr Churcher stared at his hands as if for the first time he realised they were holding nothing.

Kate Grenville

FROM *LILIAN'S STORY*

No Fury Like a Father's

Duncan did not meet Father, but saw him. From our height in the tree, Father was puny and stalk-like. Duncan was not impressed. *So that's the old bloke!* he said, without admiration. It was pointed out to Father that his daughter was in the tree above and he craned up, shading his eyes with his hand. He said nothing, turned away, walked over for a scone, and left.

Lilian, you disgust me, he said later in his study. He was a cross silhouette in front of his window. *Up a tree with a lout from the bush, even if he will be rich.* He turned away and opened the small window as if suddenly stifling. *Showing the world your drawers.* He could not fasten the catch, and flung the window out in the end so that it swung in a frenzy and banged against the frame. *Has someone told you that that is the way to catch a husband, showing him your vile drawers?* I said nothing and hoped he would lose interest, but he tore at the trousers around his crotch, loosening something, and went on and on. *What do you think you are up to? What are you up to, up there?* Finally I tried to answer. *I am not up to anything,* I said. *With him or anyone.* But Father could not accept this. He had not heard me, and began to bellow, *I will not have it!* But was there anything he could do? *I could forbid you, Lilian, to go at all,* he pointed out more calmly, and sat at his desk. I could see the light from the window pink through his ears. *But it is your future at stake there.* If I had thought that was my future, I would have rowed the old boat out into the middle of the bay and somehow made myself sink. I would have needed a few bricks, or at least pocketfuls of stones. But I knew that futures came in all kinds, and would not give up on mine just yet.

What do you get up to there? Father asked again. *Lilian, I will have answers.* The pink roses of the carpet were chaining me to the spot. I held the edge of the desk with my fingers, watching the nails go pale as I pressed harder, and wondered why it was not possible to turn away, leaving Father's question hanging in the air of this stuffy room, and leave. I would close the door carefully behind me and seal in the unfinished questions, and Father might sit there until he atrophied, waiting for answers.

The silence finally wore me out. I was becoming bored with this room. *We get up to Shakespeare,* I said, and did not expect him to believe me. *We recite Shakespeare.* This was exaggeration, of course, since I recited Shakespeare and Duncan listened, but it saved me having to confront in Father's company the words that Duncan did recite. Exaggeration or not, it was enough to enrage Father. He rose from behind his desk and spilled the paperweights in front of him. *Shakespeare,* he snorted. *Expect me to believe that story, Lilian?* He looked at me for long enough to realise how funny I was, and began to laugh. His laughter filled the room, flattening the roses, beating at the window to get out, and I stood in front of him. *Come on, Lilian,* he said at last. Tears twinkled in the corners of his eyes and he wiped them away with a sigh. *Wonderful,* he said, *let's hear you, Lilian.* His rage and shouting could not have made me recite, but his scorn and laughter were provocations of the right sort.

I did not look at him as I recited, but at the window where a branch swung backwards and forwards, applauding. Father did not stop laughing. *Oh, Lilian,* he crowed. *You are like one of those apes, taught to do things.* Then I could not stop, but felt my mouth shaping word after word, faster and faster, and on those hated pink roses saw page after page slipping over, thick with words. *Stop, Lilian, stop!* I heard Father shouting, and felt his hands on my shoulders. *Shut up, Lilian.* His voice was only a distant interruption to the words it was vital to keep reading from the roses. When he slapped my face I saw startled points of light before my eyes and a great ringing began in my ear.

I lay with a headache like an axe between my eyes, and did not remember how I had arrived in my own room, stretched on the bed with my toes towards the ceiling, a wet cloth on my face. *You were upset, Lilian,* said Mother from a chair beside me. *And so we brought you here.* Mother's eyes wandered over my face and settled on my chin to speak to. She winked laboriously at it. *I told them it was your time of the month,* she whispered. *And they believed me.*

Healthy girls with broad feet recover from most things. It took a week or two, though, for me to find that the heavy leather Shakespeare that had been a gift from Father when I was a child had been taken away again. *Who has taken my Shakespeare?* I asked John, and he looked more stupid than necessary in denying everything. I would not cry in front of anyone so dull and mulish and did not bother to hit him. Later, though, he came to find me. *Father took the boat out*, he said, *and drowned your book*. I cried, but it did not matter, because I had enough in my head to last me a lifetime.

Scandals

Lil, they are saying you will do anything, Ursula said. *They say you are after him.* Ursula herself was not required to do anything now, and smiled smoothly at the world from safety. There was nothing Rick would not do for her now. *I am your friend, Lil, and I understand,* she said, and smoothed a wisp of hair. *I am happy, and do not care what anyone else does.* Something in Ursula was ripening and sweetening in the light of requited love. *But others are talking,* she said. *It is the business of being in the tree with him all the time.* Of course I had noticed the way they looked when we came down. They saw my flush, too, and did not know it was just from all the words I had been taught. Their faces were prettier than mine, but bitter above their voile.

A Mother's Work is Never Done

So much scandal even reached Mother as she sat with the stopwatch on the terrace. *Sit, Lilian, there is something I must say,* she said briskly, and I sat opposite her in the deckchair, and watched her face forget what she had had to say. Nodding, she followed the course of a ferry as it steamed slowly across the bay. The chair creaked under my weight and the canvas strained at its stitches, but held. Mother's eyes were fascinated by the crescents of dark cloth under my armpits. *Lilian,* she said, reminding herself who I was. *Lilian.* I could see her labouring to say something more, and at last, smoothing the stopwatch like a cat in her palm, she said, *Your brother is a boy, and girls are not like boys.* She stared at me closely as if to make sure I was following. *Yes, Mother,* I said, and waited.

Her face was hidden behind its curtain of frown and it was hard to see the face of the smiling young woman who had married Father. I had pored over those old photographs until the breath wheezed through my nose from crouching on the floor so long, trying to see something more. She had married in Valenciennes lace that curved behind her in a train like a whirlpool, and her flowers had wilted in her hands. But although I could see every bud and trace every fold of the lace, I could not see what had happened to Mother.

I was willing to blame myself. No one had warned Mother that a daughter might grow into a fat watchful girl with thick red cheeks and tiny triangular eyes. She could not have imagined that her own daughter would be so clearly unsuitable to wear the Valenciennes, now packed away somewhere in tissue paper and lavender. She would not have thought any daughter of hers could sweat so profusely, would so often have morsels of food on her clothing, would have hair the colour of buried bones and as lank as grass.

But Mother was not a shirker, and she loved me enough to try to warn me. In her thin papery cheeks a terrible flush had risen and her fingers were turning the stopwatch over and over. *Lilian, when a woman becomes a woman, there are changes.* I could not think of the words to tell her that she did not need to go on. We sat listening to a blowfly drone between us and away, and I tried to forget the way Miss Vine's face had been full of disgust, those years ago, when she had suddenly snatched at me as I ran out into the playground and hissed, *Go to Matron at once.* She had been so close to me that spittle had landed on my face, and she had been so disturbed that she had brushed it off with the side of her hand and said *sorry* as if she had forgotten who I was. *The back of your skirt, Lilian,* she had whispered at me with horror, and when I looked and saw the ugly blob of purple on the back of the green skirt, I had been horrified, too, and afraid.

I am twenty, I told Mother, and saw her flinch as if I had shouted. Had I shouted? She twisted her wedding ring as if to unscrew her finger. *That is why it is time, Lilian.* I watched her stare out over the bay. The ferry had disappeared around the headland, leaving a dirty thumbprint on the sky, and a gull was wheeling and plummeting into the water. From a bush near us a bird sang the same three notes over and over like a practising soprano. Mother's eyes glanced quickly backwards and forwards across the bay and the sky as if reading an interesting page. Her lips moved silently and her right hand sketched tiny gestures. When she turned to me again, the furrow between her eyebrows was smooth and I saw a canine catch on her lip as she smiled. *You see,* she said happily, *it is all very simple.* I nodded and said *Yes*, thinking of the hopeless feeling, standing behind the screen in the sick bay, shivering in camisole and bloomers with a thick wad of cloth between my legs. When Matron had returned with the sponged green uniform, she had stared rudely at my thighs beneath the bottle-green bloomers and I had been conscious of how mottled and dimpled they were. *Next time, Lilian, be more careful,* she had said, and watched me as I struggled with buttons.

Mother had fallen into a doze, her knuckles pink as she gripped the stopwatch even in sleep, and I left her there. Later the breeze would come across the water and blow wisps of her fine hair across her face and into her nose, until she would wake up with a jerk and the curtain would be drawn tightly back across her face. But in sleep, with her duty done by her daughter, she could be recognised as the young girl proud of her husband and her Valenciennes.

Marian Eldridge

PRIMAVERA

Aunt Chrissie Jennaway invites Alvie Skerritt down to Melbourne for the August school holidays. She's Alvie's aunt, Joan Skerritt's sister, the one who swapped country for city, and married money.

Alvie can't wait. She's fed up with this hoon town, fed up with her cranky, jangling family. What is there here that she wants to do? She knows every shop window by heart. She would like someone to talk to, maybe, but what is it she wants to say? *What?* she demands.

Her father, Ray Skerritt — he's the shop steward out at the paper mill, and he's always on about something, job sharing, industrial safety, Alvie's last maths test — he says You're off to a silly life, just don't get ideas, Alvie.

Why are men always so bossy, why can't they just leave you alone?

Alvie shrugs: I can take care of myself. Joan Skerritt, her mouth full of pins because she is hemming Alvie's new skirt for Melbourne, jabs Ray Skerritt with a look: Chrissie is my sister, Ray, do you *mind?*

Scenting battle, the little kids sparkle.

Alvie looks at her family and sighs.

. . . In what way silly, she wants to know. It's no big deal is it to want a bit of fun instead of the ever-present boiled cabbage stink of the paper mill, and a houseful of kids and trampled toys and homework and washing all over the place which as far as Alvie can see is about all that her mother has got from her father. A female's life is shithouse. So Cass Jawkins reckons. She's only in Alvie's year but she's got it sussed out: look after number one! Yeah right, says Alvie, in that sing-song surprised tone that everyone's using just now.

'Do stand still, Alv!' complains Joan Skerritt through the pins. 'Do you want me to get this hem straight or don't you?'

Alvie can't wait to get on that train.

But if the mill town's a bore, it turns out life in Melbourne is no great riot either. Dragging after Aunt Chrissie first thing to admire a floppy new pansy or a bulb poking through a mush of leaf-litter. Watching Aunt Chrissie bid for an old chair that Alvie thinks should go straight to the tip. Having cakes and coffee together in posh little shops where Alvie's appetite shrivels just thinking what her father would say about the prices. Then home to Uncle Rupert who's a prune, and that enormous squeaky-clean house where from the fancy three-piece mirror in her bedroom Alvie catches her triple image looking sideways at her homemade skirt.

What's more, because it's school holidays, any day now that wimpy kid Philip Jennaway will turn up. Philip Jennaway is Uncle Rupert's son by his first marriage. Alvie remembers Philip as one of those top-of-the-class kids too dumb not to show it. He is not due at the Jennaways' until two or three days after Alvie arrives because, Aunt Chrissie explains, his mother always makes some difficulty about his spending the entire vacation with his father. Aunt Chrissie grows quite fierce about this. 'You'd think just this once — particularly when he hasn't any brothers or sisters of his own — but she always was a selfish woman.' Suddenly she lowers her voice. 'She refused him his conjugals, Alvie.'

Alvie takes a moment to realise it's not Philip she means but Uncle Rupert, that stooped grey man who during dinner will clear his throat and hawk 'And what did you do today, young woman?'

What did you do, young woman? . . . Alvie's thoughts go skittering off to all the outings lately in the Gilberts' old panel van. Would Uncle Rupert swallow the story that the mattress Butch Gilbert has in the back is just a bit of showing-off to impress his mates? Despair like dirty bathwater washes over Alvie. She's fed up with flogging the same old line, 'Yes of course he behaves himself' to her parents, and to Butch Gilbert 'No you can't — next time maybe — right now I've got you-know-what, it's just started, I've got, you know, *Charlie.*' That's what girls have to say. He falls for it every time.

Changing out of her jeans into her skirt for dinner because that's the custom at Jennaway's, Alvie tiptoes across to the three-piece mirror. Well, Alvie? The whole room is holding its breath. Alvie holds her breath too, squeezes up her eyes, tries hard for the sting of tears in her nose — a gaggle of girls crying together, but no tears come. So she studies her reflection, trying to make sense of it, trying to put together what she sees: three skinny girls with small, tense breasts, flat stomachs, hip bones sticking out like the wings on Uncle Rupert's leather chair. And inside, under the clothes, under the skin, the secret bones and veins and pulses, pumping blood, getting ready for Charlie, holding her together but all for what? She turns slowly, raising her arms, and thinks about a picture she has seen in some art book at school: three girls, arms lifted, absorbed in movement, oblivious of gawkers, as, wearing nothing but see-through nighties, they dance barefoot in a garden. *Asking for it, got up like that*, snicker the gawkers as one of the girls gets jumped by some yobbo ... She thinks about her mother, kitchen images mostly, and that time she was pregnant with Lurlene, tight as a watermelon, you could see her navel when the wind blew her smock. In Grade Five Cass Jawkins wouldn't believe that babies didn't come out through your navel. You could laugh at Cass Jawkins then. But not now, Cass Jawkins makes out she knows everything now. And what after all is there to get so excited about, says Cass Jawkins. Just a guy slobbering on you and a bit of discomfort, a bit of blood.

Yeah, just a bit of blood, echoes Alvie Skerritt. A female's life is ruled by blood.

But what does Alvie Skerritt know about anything? She knows enough to scrape through most exams. She knows that the first Mrs Jennaway wouldn't give Uncle Rupert his conjugals and that this is a terrible thing, not natural Aunt Chrissie declares. She knows from mooching around in the garden where Philip Jennaway once built a treehouse, now abandoned like elastics or marbles. And where will any of *that* get Alvie?

Your age, Alvie, is the springtime of your life, her father tells her. Alvie reckons it's more like going into a maths test with only bits of the formulas inked onto her palm. They will all wake up to her one of these days — her parents, Butch Gilbert, knowing Cass Jawkins — and then what will she do?

Going downstairs for their pre-dinner sherry that makes Alvie secretly giddy, she finds that Philip has arrived. One glance at him and she ducks back upstairs to put on her special black lipstick. Oh golly, that Philip! My cousin in Melbourne's *gor*geous, my cousin's a real hunk o' spunk, she practises telling Cass Jawkins. 'He*llo*, nice to see you again, Alvie,' he intones, and gives her a peck on the cheek. He has a faint moustache now and he wears his hair longer, spunky, she tells Cass Jawkins. 'White, thanks, Dad,' he says in that supercool voice. Uncle Rupert pours him a glass of wine instead of sherry and he stands swirling his glass and perving over it. This so intrigues Alvie that she practises with her sherry, moving her glass under her nose as she drinks in Philip. He'd be as tall now as Butch Gilbert, not as lunky though. His wrists escape from his coat sleeves like flyaway insects; Aunt Chrissie says straight after dinner she will get to those sleeves and lengthen them. At this Philip smiles, the old smile that Alvie can handle. Draining her glass, she catches his eye and tosses him a black, giddy simper. A tic jumps at the corner of his mouth.

'Chrissie,' he says — he directs all his comments at Aunt Chrissie but keeps glancing at Alvie. 'Chrissie, this is a survival thing, did you know that given a choice, in a maze say, slaters will turn right then left then right then left?' Well gee whizz, Phil.

It is arranged that Philip will take Alvie sightseeing. Alvie sees Aunt Chrissie give Uncle Rupert a pleased little nod. Philip takes her first to the Museum, a sombre great building with a tarted-up cable tram at the entrance. Alvie's brain grows muzzy as Philip yacks on happily about the model steamships and the cutaway trains. They look at Phar Lap in a glass case. Phar Lap's coat gleams and muscles ripple as though he wants nothing better than to burst through the glass and gallop out of that winter-still room. Philip explains that his heart which was more than twice the weight of that of a normal horse is displayed miles away in the National Capital. Alvie looks from the dead gleaming horse to Philip and sees that little tic jump again when he catches her watching him. She wonders if he has ever kissed a girl. When they come out at last into the spring sunshine which has cast a sherry-coloured glaze over everything, she takes hold of his hand, and keeps hold of it all the way home in the tram.

Back in the Jennaways' garden, she tells him she has something to show *him* — and she takes him through the tangled prunus and flowering currants to the platform constructed in the big leaning wattle. 'My old treehouse!' he says wonderingly.'I made it years ago out of some bits of timber left over from something but I can't recall playing in it much.' Climbing up, he leans down to give her a hand but she laughs and pulls herself up. Twigs catch at their hair. They sit down. She puts her arm around him and leaning her head against his jumper, listens to his heart busy in its own secret world. 'I don't like cold dead places with old dead horses without hearts,' she mutters.

'What did you say? I can't hear you.'

For reply she raises her face and runs her tongue over his ear. He shudders, his lips touch hers. He tastes nice, she decides, better than Butch Gilbert or Herbie Mason who mash your face with their demanding smoky tongues. After a while she sits away. 'Let's leave some for tomorrow,' she says faintly.

The next day, and the next, and the next, they hurry home from the Art Gallery, Myer's Bargain Basement, a second trip to the Museum. When his tentative hands have gone far enough for that day according to the code of the girls back home, she draws back and asks him things about himself. Get them talking, says Cass Jawkins, it gives you a breather. But Alvie surprises herself by actually listening. Back home she never listens to Herbie or Butch. Philip says he doesn't know much about girls. He envies her, going to a mixed school. There's a girl on his tram but he doesn't know how to start off and anyway it doesn't matter now, does it? He envies people like Chrissie and his father, and now the Skerritts; some people are just lucky, able to love, he was coming to believe he was one of those people destined to miss out on all that.

What a screwed-up life! Alvie feels a pang of affection for that boring, bossy, jostling family back home.

'Does your mother have a boyfriend?' she asks one afternoon.

Philip shrugs. 'She's always going to the theatre and things with people — men — but she says they're all pigs. I guess that means me, too. She's joking of course but you know what? — she used to complain if Dad so much as came into the bathroom when she was having a shower.'

'What was he trying to do? Pinch her bottom?'

'Maybe.'

At this incongruous view of Uncle Rupert, Alvie laughs. She has a quick picture of herself: soap up to the chin in the old crazed bathtub at home, and in bursts Gorgeous to pinch her bottom — Who? David Bowie? Prince Andrew?

'Aren't you glad I'm not one of the museum pieces, Phil?' she asks, nudging him.

She is not prepared for what happens next. It's as though some crazy kid has thrown himself into Uncle Rupert's leather armchair and flung it over backwards. 'I could rape you, you know!' he blurts. As she twists her head angrily, thinking What a dumb thing to say, he throws himself off her, crying 'Help me, Alvie! I don't know what I'm doing, I'm so crazy for you — I feel ashamed but why *should* I feel ashamed, you don't, do you? But then you're not a rapist, are you? My mother reckons a fellow that does that to a girl against her will deserves the knife.' She would, thinks Alvie. 'Maybe we'd better stop coming here — yes, that's the only thing, Alvie, stop coming here, stop kissing, stop going around together to museums and things.'

Alvie sits up and brushes twigs and wattle bloom off her coat. 'Aunt Chrissie will think we've had a fight,' she says slowly. It's as though someone has copied out the right formula and passed it to her under the desk. She says, bending down to him, 'Do you really want to? Stop coming here, I mean? They haven't planned anything for us for tomorrow, Phil.' And watches her hand run over those forlorn shoulders until he turns to her, saying 'You know I don't!'

'So . . . no more attempted assault, huh?' she jokes, but her voice sounds strange, dazed. Tomorrow she will know as much as anyone — her mother, Cass Jawkins. 'Only you'd better get something,' she continues. 'You know — get something? Glad-Wrap, that'll do.' So Cass Jawkins reckons.

But next morning she wakes with a familiar drag in the pit of her stomach, a heavy, fat cramping, and hurrying to the bathroom to make sure, she flies into a rage against all those forces — Butch Gilbert, Cass Jawkins, her own body — that are pushing her into this thing with Philip and then at the last moment like a stupid joke shoving Charlie in the way.

Perhaps Philip won't want to today, she thinks — perhaps he's forgotten — but no, when they set out at Aunt Chrissie's suggestion for a picnic in the Botanic Gardens, he turns aside at the Jennaways' front gate and pushes through the shrubbery to the treehouse. Savagely she thrusts aside his hand and climbs up by herself. 'Philip,' she says, and now she is nearly crying, Alvie Skerritt caught cheating at last. 'Listen, about us — there's *Charlie*.'

'Charlie?' Philip frowns, drawing away. 'Charlie?' At this reaction Alvie is offended. Because it's something that happens to half the world, isn't it? Just because *he* doesn't, he needn't back off as though she's diseased. She is so angry that she fails at first to take in Philip's hurt protest: 'You didn't tell me — only of course there would be, wouldn't there, lots, I suppose, queues — droves — I guess I was just an amusement.'

She is too busy saying caustically 'Charlie's not my

favourite friend, actually. Nor anyone's.' At this point she realises Philip's mistake, and laughs. Philip says 'Actually I don't much like two-timing myself' and tries to shake off her hand when she takes hold of his arm.

'Relax, relax,' she soothes, much as her mother soothes her father when he's tensing everyone up about bombs or green belts or something. 'I can't help it, truly I can't.' She takes a deep breath. (A female has to make the most of these things, Alv.) 'That Charlie gets around — more than you ever will, Phil. He's what you might call unavoidable amongst the girls I hang around with.'

'All of them?'

'All of them. Sooner or later.'

Without another word Philip jumps down from the tree-house. Then, because he is a courteous boy brought up to help women, he turns back to assist Alvie. But refuses to look at her. So this time she takes his outstretched hand, and when she is standing on the ground again, sways against him. Puts her arms around him. Observes the familiar tic begin to twitch at the corner of his mouth. As soon as he kisses me, she tells herself, slipping her hands under his jumper, Just as soon as he kisses me I'll tell him what Charlie really is. Her hands move up and down that resisting back. But he has to kiss me first.

Barbara Hanrahan

IDA SPIDER

The men used to laugh at her because she was always pregnant. But once, when everybody thought she was going to have another baby, she got very sick and was sent down to the Hobart Hospital. They operated and removed a large tumour, and some nurses vomited when they saw it — it was like a plum pudding, full of bits of everything she'd eaten.

She was my stepmother, I was reared by her. My father married her thinking she'd look after us four girls, but she didn't, she was cranky. She belted us with the pot stick, the broom and anything she could get hold of. She kept having children but Freddy died, Jimmy died, Peggy died and Milly died. Nelly and Harry lived and were red-headed but Harry put Oil of Roses on his hair to make it dark.

I was six when my real mother died. Her name was Edith Mary, she had beautiful long black hair but was crippled and didn't go out much. She had arthritis very badly for a long long time and Dad spent lots of money on her, trying to get her better. She had an invalid chair and an electric belt and all sorts of things but the doctor couldn't do any good for her. She died soon after my little sister, Sarah, was born.

My two older sisters were Ellen and May. We lived in Bagdad, Tasmania — about twenty-five miles out of Hobart. Bagdad had been named by the explorer who went round with a copy of the Bible and *The Arabian Nights*. It was full of apple trees and Dad worked for the sawmill at Barber's Marsh, carting timber for the apple boxes to the orchards. He'd made his cart from gum trees and worked very long hours. He harnessed the horses at three o'clock in the morning and made for the mill along awful country roads.

My stepmother had great big bosoms and ginger hair she did in knobs over her ears. She cooked roasts and meat pies and when we had no meat we'd chop the head off an old fowl that had finished laying. We used to have pastry made out of dripping, and she made pickles and the plum jam we had in our sandwiches for school. There were kangaroos in Bagdad, way out in what they called the Hunting Grounds, and Dad went kangaroo shooting once a year. Then my stepmother made kangaroo patties and kangaroo stew.

Dad had sideboards and a moustache and a black and white dog with a white tail. One day he tripped over the dog and broke his collar-bone and the bone went right through the skin; they took him to the doctor and a man held him while the doctor pushed the bone back into place. Dad was all tied up with bandages and my stepmother had to shave him and she cut off his moustache and sideboards.

Our house was built of weatherboard with a nice verandah and we had a lavatory out the back you put ashes in. We had about ten acres and Dad planted a few fruit trees by the house and grew vegetables. My stepbrother brought seedlings home from Mr Butler's garden and he grew tomatoes, Chinese cabbages and green cauliflowers, but his parsnips were so big nobody would buy them. We had blackcurrants and raspberries and there were roses up the path, a red one and a Cloth of Gold. One winter there was snow like cottonwool on the roses, and then that summer it was so hot and dry our heels went down the cracks in the ground.

The horses were called Blossom, Gyp and Prince, but we weren't allowed to play with them because they did enough work without carting us kids round. We plaited red, white and blue ribbon through their manes and tails, and Blossom and Gyp won first and second prize in the Kempton Show for a plough team. We had two cows my stepmother milked, and the dairy up on the rise gave us the calves they didn't want and we'd fatten them up and sell them. We fed skimmed milk to the pig and scrubbed its back, but Dad tied up its legs and stabbed its throat and my stepmother caught the blood in a basin to make black pudding. Dad had three sandy cats —

one with a long tail, one with half a tail and one without a tail; we thought Tom was a boy cat until she had kittens.

They called me Ida Spider, but I was christened Ida Jane Smart. I was always very small and looked old; even when I went to school I looked old.

Bagdad School had two rooms where Mrs Hayes taught the small children, and her son Mr Aubrey Hayes taught the big ones. Mr Hayes had a withered arm so he couldn't use a cane, but he'd stand us in the corner to face the class and be laughed at. Mrs Hayes kept us back after school to clean her kitchen and our mothers wondered where we were. My sister and I sat beside one another, but we copied so Mr Hayes separated us and I had to sit next to one of Wilsons' girls. There was a large family of Wilsons' girls and they had a little pony and trap that seated two in front and two in the back. Their brother died and Wilsons' girls came to school dressed in deep black, not a sparkle on it, and everybody called them the Black Crows. Chambers' boy had nice brown eyes and showed us how to write with two pens to get our fifty lines for talking written faster. I wasn't allowed to skip at school because my stepmother said I'd wear my boots out.

I slept in a bed with my sisters — we slept two at the top and two at the bottom. We washed ourselves in the tub every Saturday night to be clean for Sunday. Our mother had been a Catholic so we were, too. There wasn't a Catholic church in Bagdad but Father Corcoran said Mass in Kempton every second Sunday, so we walked the three miles there and back without breakfast. We wore our best dresses and straw hats and stockings and garters, and had embroidery round our shimmies and pants. I made my confirmation at Kempton Catholic Church in a white dress and a white veil made out of mosquito net. There was incense and brass candlesticks and three statues of the Virgin. My mother was buried near that church.

Granpa Smart died of pneumonia on my birthday. Granma Smart would hit us with her walking-stick or poke us if we did anything wrong. She wore long black dresses, flannel petticoats and long drawers; she had a hairnet, a bonnet, a gold watch and a five-shilling-piece brooch. On her mantelpiece were vases and ornaments — china dogs with red ears and an old man sitting up at a table, pouring out his tea.

Uncle Frank was my mother's brother and lived with Aunty Bet and lots of children out in the bush. They knew my stepmother was cruel, so they petted me. When Aunty Bet and her daughters came down to catch the train to Hobart, they tucked their long skirts up under their belts and walked through Bagdad with their petticoats showing because the roads were dusty.

My stepmother told me I came from under a cabbage tree and I believed it, until some girls started getting their monthlies and told me different. It happened to me at school and one of Wilsons' girls went and told Mrs Hayes who came and did me up with a belt and a piece of old sheet.

Granma Smart went into a coma and died and my stepmother took her watch and five-shilling-piece brooch, her vases and ornaments. My sister, Ellen, got married at fifteen to a man named Skewes and my sister, May, cleared out and went to work as a maid. I started wearing stays that laced up at the back and I'd put the cord over the bed-post and pull it in. I got a prize at school, *The Pilgrim's Progress*, and then I left.

Soon after I left school, I went to work for the butcher's wife on Saturday mornings. She gave me a shilling to mind her four children and do the housework. I had to scrub under the carpet and even take the old coconut matting out and scrub under that.

The 1914 War came and most of the boys I'd gone to school with were killed; every time people saw the minister go into a house they'd know another boy was dead. Bagdad was a busy place with bazaars and fairs and dances in the apple shed — there were dozens of things to raise money for the soldiers.

I left home to work for Mrs Buzzacott and her two spinster daughters as a live-in maid. Mrs Buzzacott's two sons went to the War; Roy was killed and Joe came back but he went silly. Then I went to Hobart to work at the Reverend Swan's. He was good but his wife was a hypocrite. I didn't like her and she didn't like me, so I left to work at a nurses' home and was there quite a while.

Then I moved to Launceston, it was a one-eyed place, and I was only getting a few shillings a week. I wrote and asked Dad if I could leave Tasmania and go to Melbourne to see my aunt; he said I was over twenty-one and could do as I liked. The family I'd been working for in Launceston had the mumps and I had a stiff neck when I boarded the ship, but thought it was from sleeping with my girlfriend in a single bed. When I realised I had the mumps I never told anyone on board, and hid my swollen neck in the collar of my coat. Aunty was terrified Uncle would catch it when I landed in Melbourne. It was cruel having mumps in strange surroundings. I used to take a basin of water into my bedroom and bathe my neck.

I got a job as a cook for some American people at South Yarra (they were great golfers and showed me how to make a different white sauce with melted butter, and their two children ate an apple for breakfast), but decided to go on to Adelaide. It was the Depression and on the train people said I wouldn't get work, but I found a job a couple of hours after arriving, through the Employment Office in King William Street. Mrs Garratt from the Austral Hotel, who'd been looking for a waitress, took a fancy to me.

The day I started at the Austral, Flavell's canvas goods store opposite caught fire and hundreds of rats came across to the hotel. There were rats everywhere. They jumped out of the bread bin and we had to take care where we stepped.

The last waitress hadn't done her work properly and there were still dirty butter dishes on the tables, but it was a nice hotel. I had a white apron and cap and a black dress with long sleeves. The people from up the river stayed there when they came to the city and there were four boarders, all shop assistants at Foy & Gibson's. It wasn't hard work but it was busy; I got thirty shillings a week. Mrs Garratt kept a full staff through the Depression. There was a kitchen-maid, a cook, a waitress, a relieving maid, a housemaid and three barmen.

The Austral had a big lounge where girls came to have a drink and find men to take home — they were lounge girls. There were white linen tablecloths in the dining-room and curls of butter in silver dishes. I had to roll the butter and make it curl and decorate it with parsley. I bought a root of parsley and planted it in the Austral's back garden, but they reckoned if you grew parsley you'd have an increase in the family so Mrs Garratt pulled it up.

There was a man called Archie staying at the Austral. He had a hump on his back from the War — he'd been gassed and shell-shocked and buried. He'd lost his speech, he could just whisper, and even the doctors in London couldn't cure him. He had bad nerves — if a motor car blew its horn he'd fall over in the street. He was a contractor from up north, who'd go out and build a fence, sink a well, make a tank; and he'd get scrap metal, beer bottles, anything he could find, and bring them down to Adelaide in a lorry. I felt sorry for him, and when he went back north we started to write.

He came down to the Austral twice a year, and in between we kept on writing. We wrote for years but he never mentioned marriage. Eventually, he got me a job at a hotel in Hawker, near the sheep station where he was working.

You could see the dust coming along the hill towards the hotel. We got up at four o'clock to do the washing, but before we could get it off the line it was khaki, the colour of a biscuit. I was up there six months and there was a dust storm every day, it never rained. I never saw a pattern on the lino for dust, and we had to cover up the jugs and basins in the bedrooms.

Archie would ride a horse down from the sheep station to see me and one day I told him I wasn't going to stop there, I was going back to Adelaide. He asked me to marry him and said he could get me a job cooking for the six men in the shearers' quarters at the station.

We were married in the priest's house at Hawker; we were both over forty. I wasn't going to tell anybody, but Archie had a few drinks and went round telling everyone. I wore a navy costume and a crocheted hat that had once been white (it was a biscuity colour from being in the shop-window so long, and they let me have it cheap).

I didn't know he was a born and bred alcoholic. He wouldn't go anywhere unless he had his kitbag full of grog. He went silly when he got drunk, he didn't know what he was doing. He wouldn't go to the lavatory; he peed against the wall in the bedroom, he peed against the wardrobe and it lost all its varnish. They often brought him home and put him in the gate; he'd fall over and stay there, so I'd go out and put a pillow under his head and cover him with a rug. He should never have got married. We were too old to have children, thank God.

We moved from place to place in a truck. You can rough it, put up with it for a time, if you're getting somewhere but we never got anywhere, we were always in debt. He wouldn't bother looking for a job and if they offered him a job to do the fencing he wouldn't take it, he wouldn't work for a boss — he was his own boss.

Once when Archie was sinking a well we lived in a hut made of gum branches, but mostly we lived in a tent. When we were camped in a sandy creek bed at Sliding Rock, we woke in the night to find it had flooded. Archie caught two wild cats that were covered in rabbit fleas; I washed them in kerosene and they went mad because it burnt them, but we had them for fourteen years.

We camped at a place that was roaming with donkeys. One donkey put up its ears and looked at Archie and he shot it right through the forehead. The cats ate so much of the donkey their stomachs were swollen like puddings. Next morning only the bones were left; crows and foxes had eaten the rest.

Archie shot kangaroos and foxes and sold the skins. He skinned them with his pocket-knife and sometimes I'd see a baby kangaroo, just moving on its mother's skin — a little tiny thing, no bigger than the joint of a finger. A kangaroo is very mysterious. Archie trapped rabbits; they didn't die, poor things, they lay with their paws in the traps. Archie took his truck to pieces and left the nuts and bolts on the running-board; he went to have a cup of tea and when he came back the emus had eaten them. An emu is very inquisitive — one died through eating a bolt.

We were so much in debt, Archie had to take a job in the railways at Quorn, inspecting the carriages and trucks. We rented a house, but the landlady was an old devil who put the rent up and wouldn't let us use any rainwater from the tank to water Archie's tomatoes. I worked in the railways, too, cleaning the carriages. We stayed there ten years and then the railway bypassed Quorn, so Archie got a transfer to Port Augusta. He spent his money on drink, but I'd managed to save three hundred pounds, so I bought a house across the road from the railway. If I had any visitors, Mrs Odgers next door would go into her bathroom and listen through the thin wall. The woman the other side was good-hearted, but her husband beat her. Archie's sister, Jean, lived up on the rise; she was married and had a boyfriend who was a barman, pot-bellied, with no teeth.

I had nothing to do at Port Augusta, so I put an ad in the paper saying I'd do laundrywork. The Mission answered, and sent me teachests full of the Aborigines' shirts and dresses. I washed and ironed them, and charged so much an article. When Jean saw the Mission's cheque she was jealous, but she wouldn't recognise me in the family because I did laundry-work for the Aborigines.

Archie got put off the railways and I said we'd go to the city to live. Jean said I was signing his death warrant, taking him down there. With the money from the house at Port Augusta, I bought a neglected house in Adelaide. It was beside a rubbish dump, but it had almond trees in the back-yard, and I planted roses and a hedge.

I went out cleaning four hours every day, I worked for some real society people in beautiful new homes. They had gardeners who wouldn't do any work — they'd just lean on their shovels, and some came back at night to rob the houses. They had vacuum cleaners that plugged in, and I just had to press a button.

One day Archie went to the races and won seventy pounds, then got so drunk he fell and hit his head on the bumper-bar of a car and was taken to hospital. I went to see him three or four times before he died. They took him back to Port Augusta in a hearse, but I didn't go to the funeral. I'd seen him on the viewing table in the hospital and he looked as if he was just going to sleep.

I've been nineteen years a widow, managing on my own, I was eighty-five last September. My prayers are always answered — I've lived all these years. I go to sleep with my rosary beads in my hand (they're mother of pearl, luminous, so I can find them in the dark) and I say prayers if I can't sleep. I've got a framed picture of Pope John — him and I talk together, and I thank him for everything he's done. I've got the Last Supper on a china plate and a Sacred Heart over my bed and a crucifix over the mantelpiece and two Virgin statues. I've got a friend in Canada and every time she writes she sends me a sacred picture. If the world was at peace the weather would be better.

My right leg gets a cramp and I don't know if it's getting better or worse. I sat down on a chair in the bedroom and got tangled up in it. I fell off one of the new buses and grazed my shin, I forgot the step was there. My legs are a purplish colour.

I reckon it was a Christian Brother that brought that boy to cut my lawn, because he had that silver thing on his collar back to front. The nun at the Queen of Angels Church said he wasn't a Christian Brother but I recognised him, and I don't think the Christian Brothers are any better than anybody else today. The boy came back the next morning and wanted five dollars. I said, 'You won't get a cent, I haven't got it.' He said, 'You've got your pension cheque,' and I was after the broom — I was going to bash him with the broom;

he knew it and pushed me in the bath, and he pinched my pearls and my beads and all my earrings and all my brooches, and he ransacked the drawers and stole my handbag. I could have got out of the bath if I'd calmed down, but I didn't calm down, I yelled all day till the man next door heard and got me out.

They took me to hospital to fix my leg up and the nurses had nice soft hands. I mustn't dare rub it, but I gave it a good hot bath the other night. The Italian lady up the street's got a heart of gold but she doesn't suit me. She pulled up my flowers when I was in hospital and had a bonfire; her dog, Tiny, tore my fox skin to pieces. I've got boomerangs over the mantelpiece as well as a crucifix, and a picture of the Queen on a tray over the stove. Meals on Wheels comes and gives me good food, substantial, but they don't come at weekends so then I usually have a piece of corned beef. I don't think tea does you any good, because I wake up in the night — sometimes I get out of bed in time.

I was going through the cosmetics at Myer's and I said I'd never used lipstick and she said, 'Time you did.' I use rouge and I had my hair tinted the other day at Arturo Taverna's in Currie Street.

I love cream cakes, lamingtons and sponge cake but I've lost weight in the face and everywhere — I didn't used to have this drawn look. I've lost it round my breasts and now my brassieres are too big. My memory went after I had that blackout. I don't know, I think somebody donged me. I don't know, I don't know anything. If you tell me we'll both know.

Suzanne Falkiner

MY GRANDMOTHER THE SOCIOLOGIST

In 1925 my grandmother Ethel, then forty-six, took herself on a voyage to the United States on board the RMS *Maunganui*. By now an experienced traveller, having set off around the Pacific in 1916 and to Africa in 1920, she reported to her husband in her first letter home that the voyage to date had been unmarred in its tranquillity, and that the ship, its officers and passengers were all of the very best.

For three weeks, Ethel continued, they had trailed a wake of pearly foam across the blue and silver, and now they were in Papeete, Tahiti, where she felt able to comment on the general inability of the French to make successful colonists. The amalgamation of the European and the Polynesian was a pitiful combine, according to her observation; the virtues of both had gone and the vices flourished. The European had introduced mosquitos, bicycles, sewing machines, telephones, corrugated iron, syphilis and influenza — in all, a bag of mixed blessings.

Ethel had strolled along the main street of the town, which ran parallel to the beach and was lined with scarlet Flamboyants, to the big white *bastille*, or prison, and to the hospital, also white; the club; the Post and Printing Office; the bank; past the two laundries and the white cathedral with its blue roof, to the Governor's palace.

In the side streets, shaded from the glare by the Banyan trees, she had found Chinese stores that sold silks and cottons from China, tinned meats from Chicago, and the very best Parisian toilet requisites from the houses of Coty and Morny, including perfumes, soaps, powders, lipsticks and kohl.

As a result of this, she went on, the native girl was indeed a quaint addition to the landscape after she had applied a generous coating of rose or mauve *poudre-de-riz* to her dusky skin, along with the aforementioned lipstick and kohl.

Papeete itself was most beautiful at night, when the darkness fell suddenly and the moon had not yet risen. Then, Ethel wrote, it was necessary to feel your way along the streets in the gentle coastal breeze, hearing only the soft pad of naked feet in the dust to indicate that life continued. Then, also, the air was spicy and filled with the sound of a million million cicadas.

These last, she noted, competed with the military band that played at 9 pm all the year round on the grassy square in front of the Governor's palace, and it was 'even money' which might prevail.

At eleven the monstrous tropic moon rose out of the sea, illuminating all the tiny houses with their white fences trailing lianas. A few yellow gleams of lamplight shone faintly here and there and at intervals in the music one might hear the Chinese and the Tahitians chattering volubly in French with all the essential gestures of hand and arm.

There were also in evidence, she continued, a good many dingy oriental and native cafes, lighted with oil lamps and reeking with smoke and smelly foods. Men and women sat at wooden tables, and music droned through the open shutters. Depending on the predominant nationality of the *clientele*, it might be the monotonous throb of an Indian drum, the shrill screech of the Yankee saxophone, or more often the lilting Tahitian sing-song.

On a midnight stroll — escorted by her friend Mrs Beswick — Ethel had passed many small private domiciles overgrown with vegetation; doors agape, shutters flung wide, where Tahitian girls danced to plaintive strains from native instruments.

Here my grandmother descended at length into some technical detail. The native dancing, she noted, was what Somerset Maugham might describe as provocative — or he certainly would weave some lewd suggestions into it. Ethel considered that he might be wrong, or he might be correct, but to get on with her letter, she concluded, it seemed to consist of hip movement rather than foot movement, and all attention was focused on the haunch. This motion was circular, or rotary, and there was some gesturing of arm and shoulder which was incidental, as was a gentle slapping of the hands. The eyes of the dancer were downcast, she finished, the expression set in a languorous smile . . .

My grandmother's letters to my grandfather, typed out carefully, are bound in yellowing pages in a soft suede leather cover. As I read them, I see she has later made additions and corrections; pasting in here and there a photograph or an even more yellowed newspaper clipping. At this point, the following pages are scored out and the word 'omit' scribbled in pencil beside them.

In the passages so marked she goes on to describe yet another diminutive house, again with its shutters open to the road, its garden fragrant with drooping flowers. The house *reeked with primitive suggestion*, as she put it, and had two white rooms, with bed and pillows and sheets and coverlets of bright flowered chintz *shewing suggestively* in the yellow gleam of lamplight.

For animation, she continues breathlessly, *there was a tall, thin, sunburnt Frenchman with horrible smiling eyes watching a slim Polynesian maiden sobbing her eyes out as she lay face downwards across the couch to muffle her weeping*.

At this point, the first full stop for half a page occurs.

On a table nearby — Ethel continues — there were wine bottles and a reedy basket of golden bananas.

In the second room, also visible to the street, in the dim lamplight a hybrid harridan withered with years related stories (or so my grandmother surmised) in shrill tones to a bevy of winsome native girls who tittered their appreciation. Here again, there were wine bottles and glasses of ruby liquid.

Just at this moment the creak of shoe leather had announced the arrival of three officers from the gunboat, who greeted the girls with jest, and their merry retorts — '*Ici, Messieurs, comme nous sommes toutes belles*' — were audible both to the street and my grandmother.

At this point, just when I am worrying about what has happened to the Frenchman with the horribly smiling eyes, Ethel launches into some ferocious moralising on the hypocrisy of what the French Colonist terms '*la Mission Civilisatrice de l'Europe*' — if carnality indeed be the unexplained sin against the Holy Ghost, she adds. And what is worse, he does not deign even to draw the shutters to hide his *amours* from the street; though the Tahitian is a child of nature and of the earth earthy, and has no fidelity in love, nor sees any reason for it . . .

After that my grandmother turned her attention to the Chinese women, whom she saw passing by day in horse-drawn carriages and believed to be the chatelaines of the richer Chinese merchants. It was odd, she noted, that the Celestial lady rarely showed any sign of animation, seldom or never smiling. She wondered why, having heard that the Chinaman made a wondrously fine husband — and yet these inanimate, almost silly-faced women went their way so stolidly, so solemnly, in comparison to the Tahitians, who were always so merry and bright — in spite of their lack of morality.

Perhaps, Ethel continued, her husband would understand better the Tahitians' mental state if she were to explain that there was apparently no word for *virtue* in the Tahitian language, but rather there was a phrase, 'peu maitai', which loosely translated as 'good form'. Which, if she were candid, had always carried greater weight in even their own society than the former . . .

But by now her husband would be complaining of her cynicism, and so she would desist.

However, in closing, she would have to comment on the *allure* of Tahiti, notwithstanding its general air of decay. The words '*Fraternité*' and '*Egalité*' might well be replaced with '*Paternité*' and '*Inegalité*' in the colonial Pacific, she considered, but it was an interesting place in which to philosophise and a pleasant place in which to browse. She hoped that she might see it again, but probably would not, since pleasant things had a way of not repeating themselves.

She had been fortunate to have Mrs Beswick to moon about with at night— by day that good woman was busy sketching, she reported, but at night they had wandered around on foot together, seeing not a little of Tahitian life. Mrs Beswick was a true cosmopolitan, possed of no prejudices, no bias, open-minded, extremely intelligent and needless to say much travelled. In short, a very charming woman.

My grandmother's next letter would be from San Francisco, she predicted, which city they expected to reach in two days' time. Until then, in closing, she was her husband's very affectionate Ethel.

Patrick Rogers

THE SMALL STEEL BOX

These are the letters of Hugh Kippax. Thirty years — how else were those years spent? The reader of this collection is unlikely to emerge enlightened, and no doubt the same question must have occurred to Kippax's various correspondents. What else were the constituents of this man's life? At first one is at pains to know why this innocuous collection is called *The Small Steel Box* (ed. T. Porter, Danto Publications, Melbourne 1985). To a distant cousin in Panama he writes of orchids and little else; Nicholas Frouse, the Cambridge Renaissance scholar, received many snippets of research that Kippax had sniffed out, as he put it, 'from the dead end of my continent'; while Marie Soneux continued to receive inquiries from the inveterate Kippax about her amateur string quartet. The disembodied quality of this collection is accentuated by the fact that we do not know how (if at all) Soneux and Kippax ever met, or if the information sent to Frouse was unsolicited, or useless, or even a nuisance. Countered to that, of course, is the fact that all these letters are extant; the doodlings of cranks are rarely so comprehensively hoarded. In an age of dying correspondence, where elegance and *enthusiasm* such as this writer's are frowned upon and disparaged, these letters come like a new voice.

I find only one reference to a family amongst the first half of these letters. In a page of idle musing to a retired journalist in New Zealand (a house he seems to have visited with its outlook upon the Bay of Islands), Kippax wonders why it is that people eat apples in different ways. He tells us that he bites into the equator first of all, makes a circle, and then removes the northern hemisphere segment by segment, then the southern, and then cleans up the poles. He describes the whole process as methodically, no doubt, as he carried it out. His wife, however, bites at random, sometimes no two bites next to each other, and this, he informs his correspondent, after twenty years still bothers him. It is the only reference I can find to his wife in the first half of these letters which have been uncritically assembled in chronological order.

Some of the early correspondents receive only one letter and are never considered again, while to others over the decades an opus of confessions is gradually sent. (Perhaps even exchanged, but we do not know; the editor, an over-considerate friend, no doubt, certainly no professional, never enlightens us.) To Gerald Middleton, an acquaintance who lived in the Western District of Victoria and who rarely travelled to Kippax's home town of Melbourne, he gradually opened out, adopted the tell-tale slangy tone that the reader soon realises is a signal to a more personal disclosure. He repeats the anecdote of the apple to Middleton; this is a letter five years after the New Zealand one: obviously it is still bothering him. And most significant of all, only to Middleton does he go over the track of his life and question it. 'Without a doubt,' he writes early on, 'I viewed my career, the drollery of merchant banking, as a means of quickly gaining wealth, gaining property and income, and by that means *gaining time*.' He never seems to have doubted the equation that *money is time*. He repeats the formula often. I have never been to Melbourne, nor Australia of course, but he conjures up in these letters a delightful world of antipodean charm, clean affluence and comfort, a world of calm and ease. He holds no complicated European qualms about his wealth. 'It's what I set out to do, Gerald, and it is the product of no one's labour, no one's *time*, except mine.'

Upon retirement, though, at fifty he comes out with the question: 'Now — what do I do now with this time?' It is a question that the attentive reader would have seen looming ten years before. The art of the discursive chat is honed in the letters to Middleton, and sentence by sentence we start to suspect that the questions he has raised have been deeply based on the precepts by which he has ruled his life. 'I now have time to inspect my roses, a morning circumnavigation of my garden, and time to play and replay my Gluck and Ravel, or stroll down the Strand and pick up my newspapers, but why is it, in essence, that I acted to commandeer this much time?'

It is no surprise to us when these questions erupt. It is more than the pitiful complaint of an early retiree, common enough; this man worked for this moment for as long as he, and we, have known. Is man work? Nothing more than a reification of a lust for occupation? By no means is Hugh Kippax an amateur. He has read Marx, at least in part. Is this usual for a Melbourne merchant banker? He knows Adler, John Dewey, Pareto, quotes Russell's *In Praise of Idleness* to an old expatriate Britisher in Malaya to whom he was writing during the upheavals of Independence. 'If you are looking for the perfect spot for retirement, and I appreciate why you look upon England now as a foreign country, have you ever thought of Mallorca . . .?' How is it that without a skerrick of biography we do not believe that he is talking through his hat?

The question, like a goldfish surfacing through murk, grows clearer. 'Greetings from this upholstered exile!' he heads one letter. But exiled from what?

He lives in the bayside suburb of Williamstown, a district apparently separated by industrial murk and geography from the city, and on the waterfront where he lives he watches Korean or Liberian tankers and merchant vessels, vast rusted hulks, slip through the narrow water-lane amongst the moored yachts and motor launches. Beyond this foreshore, he describes in one letter, there is the profile of the city, 'another world of glass and concrete, *my* world and yet not . . .' He enjoys the separateness. 'Divorced physically, I am now in that metaphoric state of disconnectedness, a bank account that no one has claimed . . .' It is one of the few places of the few personal comments where the self-mockery, the irony, wears thin.

Of course, these few personal touches are rare diamonds studded amongst the gravel. He frequently adopts the passive to avoid personal pronouns; it becomes obsessive. There is a series of a dozen letters to a cat breeder in California about Cornish Rexes. He has acquired two (although we suspect that his wife was the instigator) and he details their steely aloofness, the playfulness that is offered almost in the manner of a disdainful tip, their susceptibility to certain complaints, and he asks dozens of questions. Does Hugh Kippax get his answers — *did* he? We are left to decode his side of the conversation, and he rarely allows himself to be testy with his correspondents.

Then, like a bomb, his wife comes into the picture. 'Gail is ill,' he writes to Middleton. The nature of the disease is never made plain though there can be little doubt that it was cancer. It is peculiar how much of a shock this revelation is to we who hardly knew of her existence, nor even of Kippax's attitude to her. Not enough is known to condemn him with the fact that two days after he first informs Middleton of his wife's illness he is jovially writing to a relative in Sydney about a sculpture exhibition he had been to: '. . . and in one corner something that looked like viscera, something fluid, which apparently every hour was stirred up by a man (the artist!) who arrives in top hat and tails to carry out this essential element of chance. The event was not witnessed (artist meets artifact! what a horrible thought!) but a note in the catalogue solemnly advised against viewing this figure as external influence, who, in fact, should be viewed as a fundamental element of the sculpture. Are we too old for this? No, that is the easy explanation. Are the times out of joint, values distorted? It's alarming to know that just such an accusation is made every generation as its members approach my age — and yet . . .' Unlike Kippax's relative we know what Kippax knows. We learn to interpret empty asides ('it is awkward to get out these nights', '. . . perhaps we'll move . . .', 'lack of sleep is a bonus offering me even more time . . .') as having an unspoken weight of circumstance behind them. How these letters train us!

'Out of focus, staring at the ugly rust-bucket of a

Chilean container-vessel in the waterway outside the window, staring through a blur at the ship it seems to loom into the house, to fill the window and taint all the colours. This monster has been stalled outside for a week. Perhaps there is a dock strike but not having seen a paper for that long there is no way of knowing. Turning on the radio I find my concentration dissolve. It doesn't matter. Outside, in the world, I mean, there are very obvious manoeuvres being carried out. It makes you want to cry out, like seeing a beginner's two-move combination in chess, except that this is not touching. Here I am, master of my own minutes and hours, and I feel a wildness, like a poison, stalled, but only for a minute, in my own fingers. The manoeuvres of subordination, these vast fetishes, terrifying because they are so vast, *unseen* because they are so vast, so obvious, so *conspicuous*! . . . the mechanistic future so breathtaking . . . So what if the factories churn out their plenitude, ostensibly returning time to its owners — so what if the social ego is unleashed again, harnessed, so what if nineteenth-century man is unleashed by the twenty-first century? . . .'

So what, indeed? This letter explodes, ten pages long, in a letter to Kippax's brother, to whom all previous, infrequent letters had simply been a bristle of family inquiries with one or two clichés describing his own state. What drove Hugh Kippax to put down this almost Blakean treatise, and send it, and yet follow it the next day with an encouraging note to an old school friend who had been playing with the idea of starting an avocado farm? Two days later he informs Middleton that his wife was very low after the effects of chemotherapy. 'Somewhere,' the letter to his brother had argued, 'we track down the source of our drives, and say, ah, *here* we went wrong, *here* we made a wrong turn . . . choices are not increased, they are simply disguised, with one or two knocked off for good measure. I can't explain. I stand here and see absolutely how each one of us is broken down into our little box, allowed as release to form couples perhaps, and if our distress grows too intense we are allowed an individual therapy, and then returned to our small steel box.'

We are drawn into the unlit Edwardian house in

Williamstown. A well-to-do, well-educated man stands in the comfortable, *tasteful* living room. Dusk fell an hour before but he has still not switched on the lights. An ostensible life of success, of wide interests, of *extensive* enthusiasms, ends up in this darkened room. He can see the lights that festoon the container-vessel and twilight has disguised its dilapidation. It looms high and it is difficult to believe that the water there has the draught deep enough for the ship to advance. The man has time up his sleeve. It has been the imperative of his life, his successful warm life, where ease and comfort have been the constituents. He is a man of habit, conscious of the traps of the habitual. A popular figure in the local shops. In a minute he will go up the stairs, wincing at the twinge to his sciatic nerve, and look in on his sleeping wife. In a minute he will turn on the lights.

'Is it true,' he asks Marie Soneux in Montreal, 'that you gave up your job to care for your ailing sister?' A tone of wonder, or hope, enters this letter. To another he muses: 'What does a pauper possess to renounce in order to prove a sacrifice?' Do we really believe that this animal endured his decades in the boardroom, his mind intact, his *soul* intact? Early on some of his letters had been to business colleagues with only a residual personal element. Financial advice. He correctly foresaw the late-seventies collapse of the futures market; he discouraged an apparently rabid nephew from sinking his savings into some folly. But in the end the letters have moved closer to home, to the dark sombre Edwardian home that looks over Melbourne's Port Phillip Bay, and to the man whose time had been paid for with the performance of his respectable life. Why these letters? Are they a symptom? Why were they collected? The introduction (which, of course, I did not read until, in a state of hushed perplexity, I had finished the last of the letters) is less than helpful, it is infuriating. It mostly concerns itself with the editor's own problems. Who is Terence Porter? We do not know and just wish him out of our way if he is to be no help to us. We return to the final letters.

'A morning in the attic, sorting Gail's things . . .' This is three months after his wife's death. There were no letters announcing the fact; it became past history in those from a month afterwards. 'All of her clothes and things downstairs are long gone, of course — her sister came and dealt with that side of it for me.' For the first time a glimpse of a helpless man. '... maybe I'll come and visit you, Gerald, when the weather cools. We two chattering currawongs. The house here oppresses me in autumn ...' Is a tone of aged complaint entering here? 'These confounded steps! Do you know that yesterday I counted my ascents and descents? Fourteen — of both. Ridiculous. What on earth is up there to compel me up, and once up what on earth is there to force me down again? ...' He describes the walk along the waterfront where the midweek yachtsmen sort their gear, past the boat club, the cannon and the giant rusted anchor welded in place as a public memorial to something, past the neat Victorian homes that a new generation are 'doing up'. He buys a little drawing of a possum, an early work of a now establishment artist — an exorbitant price, he exclaims, 'because this fellow now has all the encrustations of success, but do I get any of that success in this little drawing? Of course not.' But clearly he is amazed at the youthful insouciance with which he hands over six hundred dollars.

There is a huge closed-down power station complex nearby, and he walks around its locked gates in an odd mood. 'The high chimneys, the cataracts and concrete and piping,' and he wonders what this huge dinosaur will be turned into. Land too costly to ignore; 'it is the curse of plummeting too quickly into the future that what one generation puts up is to be wrecked by the next. Even the gentrified Victorian homes of Williamstown I do not see as a constancy. Here this mechanic giant, a tumbling keep, but a dead weight. The air smells of dust, like pollen. The railway tracks rust. Not apocalyptic revelations, Gerald, perhaps no more than the musing of a new widower ...' *Debellatum est*. Or is it? This is the last letter in the book. Was it the last he wrote? What did Hugh Kippax do with the time he had assiduously accumulated? We never know, and the strength of these letters written by someone who has no place in the cultural or 'celebrity' world is that we are frustrated and irritated by our ignorance. It is the lesson this magnificent collection teaches us. '... probably I'll die with this old power station mothballed around the corner still. In many ways it would be a shame to pull it down, it is so Victorian, so utilitarian still, so ... Roman. At the end of every winter I'll come out of my lair and in spring sunlight sniff around its outer walls. A recurring blight — like Paterson's curse.' The editor, of course, has let so many esoteric references pass uncommented upon, and this is no exception. What is Paterson's curse? An Aboriginal hex laid upon his district? Australian slang for his sciatic problems? At the centre of such a deep and strenuously obtained knowledge of this wise, sane man we are always reminded of our benighted state.

John Clanchy

THE ART OF WRITING DANGEROUSLY

'To think you could do this to your own mother. It's an absolute disgrace.'

'For God's sake.'

'What will they say? What on earth can they think?'

'Who?'

'My friends. Who did you imagine?'

'But, Mum, for the four hundredth time, the story's not about you. It's an invention.'

'It's about a mother, isn't it? You wrote it, didn't you? Who else could it be about?'

'Mum, seriously ... No, seriously now, does it sound like you? Just listen. Will you please put that hanky away for one minute and listen?' He picked up the magazine in which the story had appeared. The margins were heavily annotated in red, the print blurred with salt water. He struggled to find the exact passage he wanted. 'Here's where the woman first comes into the story. OK? This is the first time she appears:

'Few could now detect any trace of those passions, the heedless rages which had made her beauty such a danger to all in her youth. Her hair was silver, almost white in places . . . '

'There!' she stabbed an accusing finger at him. 'Search all you like. You'll not find a single white hair on my head.'

'Exactly, Mum. Ex-actly!'

'Well, then, why do you write these things about me if they're not true?'

'Jesus.' He moved the Kleenex in range of her groping hand.

'You just do it to spite me. Out of sheer perversity.'

'Perversity?'

'Which reminds me.' The end of her nose was beginning to glow. 'The language in that story . . .'

'Look,' he rushed to cut her off, 'I knew that'd upset you. That's why I tried to explain before you even saw it.'

'Thank God your father's not still alive. This'd kill him.'

'It's realism. I'm trying to show what life's really like. I don't choose the language people use. If they use four-letter words . . .'

'But that one. Vagina, if you must. I could have put up with vagina.'

'What?'

'Spock always said use the proper terms. Even from the earliest age. Vagina . . .'

'Mum, it's got to be seen in context. Take vagina . . . Oh here, please don't start again. Look, let me try and explain. At this point in the story the boy is full of rage. The demonstration he's leading has just been stopped from entering the building.'

'Breasts . . .' she remembered. Stretching for a tissue.

'He's frustrated, completely out of control. He's not going to rush up to the nearest policeman and shout Vagina! in his face, is he?'

'Anus.'

'It wouldn't make sense.'

'Penis. Though your father was always less keen on penis.' She was calmer for a moment, remembering. 'He believed it might only start the girls thinking.'

At the mention of his sisters, a new wave of misery broke on her face. 'Oh, my poor Samantha,' she cried, 'she was due for promotion.'

'Is she dead?'

'What will this do to her? Everything had been going so well since her . . . the operation on her . . .'

'Quite,' he intervened, anxious to save her.

'. . . her thing-ey. And now this.'

'This?'

'The poor girl no longer knows who her real father is.'

'Mum, the girl in the story is not Samantha. The man is not Dad . . .'

'For twenty years she adored your father. I remember at the funeral: Mum, she said, a girl couldn't have hoped for a better father. And now . . .'

'The affair between the woman and her brother-in-law is an invention.'

'Now . . .' she sobbed, 'she's gone and buried the wrong man.'

'Would you like more tea?'

'God help you, that's all I can say, when this . . . this . . .'

'Story?'

'This public humiliation reaches your uncle Frank.'

'You think uncle Frank is the brother-in-law?'

'Think?' She snatched the magazine from his hands. As she read, she paused at the end of each phrase, her tone harsh, derisory:

'A man of lusts as large as his frame, he bore (a constant observer of all his burrowing pleasures) a curious mole, protuberant, tufted, staring, on the end of his . . .

'Who else could it be,' she demanded, 'but your uncle Frank?'

'But Mum, I swear I didn't know until this minute that uncle Frank had a . . .'

'How would it be . . .'

'On the end of his . . .'

'. . . if I had written a story about you? How would you feel then? If I'd told everyone that you were still in nappies at four? Bed-wetting at seven? If I went about rubbing the faces of the entire world in it?'

'The magazine's got a circulation of one hundred and ten.'

'That disgusting mess you made with the balloons at your fifteenth birthday.'

'All right, Mum. That's enough.'

'Mary Johnson . . .'

'Mum, please, I'll change it. I can see you're upset. I'll change it.'

'The nun at the bus-stop.'

'Before it's reissued.'

'Reissued?'

'Syndicated. A newspaper's bought it.'

'A newspaper!'

'I promise I'll change it. It's easy enough. You just show me the bits that ... Mum, please stop weeping. I'll shift things about, disguise them. It's easy enough. The whole thing's pinched anyway.'

'Pinched?'

'Of course. All my stories are like that. I just get bits and ... adapt them.'

'But where from? What about the affair between me and uncle Frank?'

'The Man from Snowy River.'

'Copied?' The shock had stopped her crying for the moment. 'All stolen?'

'That's right.'

'The incest? Samantha and Kerry and your father?'

'Lot's Daughters.'

'The boy and his mother?'

'It's Greek.'

She was still doubtful: 'But Kirk Douglas never took his trousers off once in that whole film.'

He got a pen and sat opposite her, just as he had when she supervised his homework years before. 'Just show me the bits you don't like.'

'Shaming the whole family like this ...' Her voice wavered and she reached for another tissue. 'You might at least have had the grace to be original.'

'Now don't get upset again, Mum. I'll do whatever you say.'

'I want you to make it so we're not recognisable.'

'So nobody will think it's you, is that right?'

She sniffled, placated a little.

'Let's go back to what I read before. When the woman first comes in, you remember? We'll do it together.

'Few could detect any trace of those passions ...'

'Affections,' she blew her nose.

'Affections.' He made a correction in the margin and read on:

'... *the heedless rages* ...'

'Girlish antics.'

'The girlish antics?' Pen poised, he waited for clarification. She was steadfast.

'... *which had made her beauty such a danger to all* ...'

'Mum? What about that? The beauty?'

'Oh, you can leave that. Leave the beauty,' she said, bursting into tears again, 'but the hair has got to be changed.'

Thomas Shapcott

THE COMPETITION PORTRAIT

None of us knew anything. I was thirteen, last year of primary school. Apart from the Viking Swimming Club where I was Junior Breaststroke Champion I existed for oblique competition with my twin. He had enrolled at the local Technical College for Saturday morning woodwork. I enrolled too; but for the art classes. I declared my difference.

Art Class. I had been a scribbler and a dabbler for years. My grandmother's cousin had a framed crayon sketch I did at eight, something dashed off in passion and boredom during an afternoon-tea visit. I think it was an elf on a toadstool. Her indulgence had ballooned in my mind despite modest protestations. I believed myself talented.

Art Class. Though I believed myself talented I realised talent was not enough. I could not draw the hind legs of animals. I could not draw faces full-on. I could not manage anything remotely like a portrait of my twin. An Elf on Toadstool (or was it a windswept line of trees? a circular Cat By Fire?) could say only so much. To develop my talent I would need some precise tuition. At thirteen I dreamed of immortalising everyone around me. The Archibald Prize for Portraiture always made newspaper headlines, even in Ipswich.

The first lesson was disconcerting: too many little kids and only three Seniors over twelve. Myself; a tight-skinned boy called Ivan Wilberforce; a Marburg girl called Minnie Wilhelmina Sophia Verrenkamp.

At thirteen nobody in your class or swimming club or art group is beautiful or ugly. They just are. Minnie was a streak. She was enduring the change out of infancy. At that stage I was taller than my twin and my hair had suddenly turned from pale, straight straw into a mass of waves, a corrugated regularity of grooves I strove in vain to plaster down with Californian Poppy and a scratchy hairbrush. No use.

You could not ignore Minnie. She was frizzle-haired and freckly, with a fringe. At our first art lesson she came up to me and boasted that her mouth was so small she could only put a teaspoon in. Her lips were big and fleshy, but the mouth itself was a tiny pout. Capable of a thin line of sarcasm, though. Her jutting chin seemed to force up the line of her nose which was almost translucent, with stretched, distended nostrils. It added to Minnie's haughty, assertive manner.

Minnie did not believe in her own ugliness.

I knew, though, that she was even odder than Thelma Quinnie in our class who really should have been in the Opportunity School. Only Ivan Wilberforce could challenge her. Ivan was willing to do that, to anyone, even Miss McNill. During that first lesson Ivan let us all know he would be a Scientist at Woomera. He could explain Einstein's Theory of Relativity. In 1948 none of us knew much about Einstein. Ivan offered to teach us.

Minnie adored him. She affixed herself to him, she made sure that her easel was next to his, she brought him icecreams (one of the foods that could easily slip into her tiny mouth), she showed him books from her home somewhere out in the German farming settlements beyond Ipswich. She brought in very strange old-fashioned engravings. Faces unbalanced and rounded with knotty chins or tiny eyes; faces beaked with hawk noses, people poked into twisted shapes, terribly realistic ugliness like half the faces in town. None of them like the Hollywood Lana Turners or Veronica Lakes we had been trained to see as beauty and symmetry.

Everything about Minnie was a sort of challenge to symmetry. She was the most out-of-symmetrical person I knew, an extreme version of everyone.

Ivan was almost as bad. His tight, yellowish skin, his huge forehead and tiny eyes behind spectacles: Ivan the

Snake we called him. He took Minnie and me to his home and showed us his collection of snakes and lizards and his long-necked tortoises. Ivan the Snake: he was delighted.

Minnie became, naturally, Minnie the Mouth. Nobody bothered with a nickname for me. Tom, they said. I learned to draw the back legs of animals. I still had trouble with people front-on.

There were only the three Seniors so Minnie and Ivan shared their treasures with me. Ivan was scornful that I did not know the difference between German Renaissance art and Italian. Michelangelo, Ivan insisted, was the greatest genius of all time, apart from Einstein and Mozart. He lectured us on the rediscovery of classical ideals of male beauty and form. Later, he delighted, with Minnie, in searching the town library for illustrations of Northern realist artists, and the creators of grotesques and horrors. Soldiers with hag chins and scrawny faces, matted hair, puffy eyes, talons and claws, Christs like pallid simpletons, freaks, monsters. Ivan found them riveting.

Minnie and Ivan grew impatient of copying cubes and balls, baskets of fruit and bearded iris lilies. Minnie began the game by drawing a green grasshopper gobbling the iris. Ivan was entranced; next lesson he brought in a Japanese print of almost identical precision: insect devouring flower. His own drawing that week was a squat toad with a jewel in its head. Miss McNill said it was 'uncanny and powerful' but suspected it was a copy. Start again, she insisted, concentrate on the cone and the pyramid; get the shading right.

The three of us began to linger around town. We were a trio. We would go to Londy's Cafe for icecream sodas. Ivan, one day, produced another drawing he had done, a Flagellation. The Christ figure was completely naked, scrawny and cavernous but with oversized genitals. Minnie said it reminded her of her little brother. We all laughed.

That it had become a competition was never admitted. The three of us turned up early for art classes. We would compare what we had created since last week. We narrowed our tastes. Our imaginations were held by the Gothic. Ivan delighted in reptiles and serpents and twisted naked bodies, sometimes bloodily wounded. His St Sebastians were not Roman soldiers or Mediterranean boys, they were creatures of bog and of cavern. My attempts were at women in shrouds, sightless witches, Beardsley vampires. Minnie's paintings were horrors of colour, not line. Yellow faces with green shadows, purple robes warring with carmine, burning eyes and half-open tiny mouths, long long fingers encrusted with ancient rings. Nightmare territory, closed in. Her paintings grew bigger and bigger, tighter and more constricted.

When we admired them she laughed, her metallic tinkle. Her small eyes glittered. The nose jerked back, her fingers darted around the edges of her soda glass. The tip of her tongue licked at ice cream.

I remember we ran into my twin, the three of us, heading for Londy's. I gave him an extravagant wave. A wink would have been more our style. Later, my parents quizzed me about my new friends.

We all entered for the *Courier Mail* Art Show. Miss McNill encouraged us. She had not approved of our extravagant fancies so began to supervise art lessons stringently. But she was drawn in — that was Minnie's achievement. Miss McNill was made one of the Londy's milk bar set, awkwardly. Although our drawings did become more decorous with Miss McNill there, Minnie grew straighter, taller, more imperious in the milk bar. The waiter was a Greek man of enormous size with an impassive moon face. When he leaned across to mop the glass table or hand us our sodas, his body heaved and buckled. He would stand behind the cash register for hours. I noted that he read books. Sometimes I caught sight of my brother outside. Sometimes I winked.

Miss McNill encouraged us to talk about our *Courier Mail* Art Show entries. We must plan. I talked of a lavish dustjacket design for an imaginary book. I couldn't think of any real book worth illustrating. In the event I did a watercolour of the local swimming hole (but without humans; it was a place where people raced, skipped, splashed, *moved.*

Moving figures were too hard). Ivan worked slowly and meticulously on a still-life: apple with serpent. Each week we admired its progress. India-ink with cross-hatching.

Minnie would not be drawn on her subject. Miss McNill showed her reproductions of Elioth Gruner and Hans Heysen. Minnie snorted. Too like our farm, she said. Painting had to be something other, something not ordinary, it had to be mysterious or thrilling or tragic or magic. Larger than life. Minnie challenged Miss McNill and Miss McNill after a few weeks tried to come up with reproductions from magazines that might tempt Minnie.

'But they're all local. I don't live *here*!' Minnie waved her thin arm around Londy's to take in the soda fountain, the sand-blasted mirrors with their fly spots and oily rainbows, the confectionery counter with its musk sticks and aniseed balls, the huge young Greek at the till, reading Eliot. 'I live here, here!' she gripped her narrow head, jamming in the thin curls, beaking up her nose.

Minnie never heard the rude catcalls of boys outside the North Star Hotel, selling the Sports Extra. She ignored the stares of everyone lined up at the bus-stop. My brother did not always hang around town after his woodworking lesson; I did not have to worry about him. There was a dinghy he had designed and was now building, every inch of it.

In that year we were together Minnie grew taller than all of us. Her ugliness was a magnet.

The day the Art Exhibition opened Miss McNill made a special arrangement for us to travel to Brisbane for the display; we would meet her in the *Courier Mail* foyer. Each had entries hung. It was a major excursion and we went by train. I had never travelled by train to Brisbane, neither had Minnie. Ivan however knew the ropes; he haunted the Ballad Bookstore, he went to matinees at the St James or the Rialto (which meant that he was a month ahead of everyone). We met up at the ticket office.

Somehow we did not come across Miss McNill. We did see our own exhibits: Ivan's black and white won second place. My watercolour looked splotchy and rough down in a corner near the floor but I spotted it instantly. Minnie had done — Ivan and I both exclaimed together — a self-portrait. That unforgettable nose, the fleshy berry lips, so narrow yet so droopingly full, and the hopeless razor chin that jutted above her long neck. Unflinchingly she had got it all down. The only fanciful part, a dazzling arabesque, was the costume. This was some sort of antique court dress: strings of pearls, rubies and jewels, a golden fleece medallion on a chain, a strange hat pinned with precious stones, Elizabethan ruffs, ermine. We admired it genuinely. Minnie shrugged. After all, she remarked, her family had links with nobility, Austrian royal blood.

I tittered. 'Royal blood! Is that how you got that mouth?'

'Yes' Minnie said simply. Then she poked her elbow at me.

'Well of course,' Ivan argued, 'Central Europeans are all Archdukes or Princes or Margraves, or Electors, or whatever. Stands to reason: their countries were so small, everyone ended up being married to one, or a cousin of one, or even an illegitimate offspring of one . . .'

But the more Minnie hinted, the more improbable it became. After all could one really believe every run-down milk farm harboured the Prince of Ruritania? The Princess Palatine? Jack Winks who sat next to me at school was a nephew of Mr Bradfield, the man who designed the Sydney Harbour Bridge. That was real fame, by association. Minnie's ancestors were more likely Breugel rustics, or Bosch witches, or the rough soldiers who diced for trinkets in the corners of Altdorfer.

'I call my portrait: The Marschallin.' Minnie stepped back from us.

We didn't have a clue what she meant. It was the first time she even hinted that her farmer parents might listen at night, not to 'Martin's Corner' or 'The Amateur Hour' or even to their cattle belching — but to whole record sets of German opera. The wide, low hills of the farmlands behind our town became tinted in an odd new light. The fat, waddling farmers who came in on weekends: we had thought them spies during the war, but they were even stranger perhaps; secret hoarders of something totally foreign: their culture. They must see even the hills and creeks differently. They must walk our town bitumen and re-create it in their own minds, perhaps more like their own villages in some imagined Europe. After all, the local names: Marburg, Minden, Engelsburg. Minnie swanked away from us. But also utterly like any plain girl near the top of the Seventh Grade after exam results are announced. Her portrait was Grand Champion.

One thing though. Over the past months I had learned to look at the townspeople, the farmers, kids in my class. They had been painted. They became interesting. Through some artist four hundred years back my eyes had been taught all these people around me had resonance, they had ancestry. I looked up to see who the Marschallin was.

But our day out together really ended the triumvirate. We had exhausted our conversation, Minnie's teaspoon-sized mouth was just Minnie's mouth, Ivan's snake head merely Ivan. I began joining up with my twin brother, after his woodwork class. We would go to the Ritz Cafe, further down the street. We won the Viking Relay later that summer.

It was thirty-five years later that Minnie accosted me, face out of a small-town boyhood in the aftermath of the war. I was in the Budapest Museum of Fine Arts, examining the alcove of Fifteenth Century Northern European schools. It was a portrait, by Barend van Orley of the Emperor Charles V of Austria, the first great Habsburg. The portrait was of a young man, with a few downy chin hairs, dressed in the gown-like robes of that time and with a jewel-encrusted fur hat, his hair cut straight across his forehead and at jaw-level, very much the hairstyle of the girls in my primary years. The mouth was marginally larger but there was that same full lip and you could almost hear Minnie's nasal twang. The chin might be stronger but there was something about the neck. And the thin, almost translucent nose, forcing the head up. In Charles all these things conspired to make the young

Emperor indeed a distinguished presence; the apparent ugliness was subsumed in a greater intensity.

It could have been Minnie's self-portrait, idealised. It could have been her twin — different, but parallel. Minnie Wilhelmina Sophia Verrenkamp. Minnie would be a moody mother by now, or a typist in some city office, or a hard-worked spinster daughter inspecting the cows for cattletick, her widowed father still tyrannical.

I returned to that portrait again and again, that day and for the rest of the week.

Brian Dibble

If I Ever Decide To Im-mo-late Myself ...

1

'*... I want to invite all my friends. But y'all better hope I start early in the morning ...*' Vic Mix said that. But since people often don't remember, and not that many people have heard of him in the first place, I'll tell something about him now before he's completely forgotten.

He was the man originally hired to paint the Opera House. The Project Managers working for the Executive Committee were astounded when his quotation came in so far below all the others. When theirs averaged about $200,000 his came in at $20,000. Since there was a joke going around about the two Irishmen who submitted a ridiculously small quote to put a tunnel under a river, the Manager felt compelled to inquire further. The joke went on: Paddy and Mick were going to start on opposite sides, digging by hand; when asked what would happen if the two didn't meet, they responded, 'Well, you'll get two tunnels for the price of one.'

Try as they might, though, the Managers could not contact Vic directly. Calls to his telephone number only reached an ersatz Dial-a-Prayer, a woman reciting the Our Father in a way presumably calculated to elevate more than just one's spiritual horizon. '... Howard be thy name, thy kingdom come, thy will be done ... For thine is the power and the glory ...' The address turned out to be a massage parlour cum religious book shop. The woman there said she did not own the place or know the owner. She had never heard of Vic Mix either. The Managers confusedly thumbed through the religious literature as they asked their questions, trying not to look at the silhouetted sign on the rear wall between two doors leading to the back. Beneath it was written, 'I am risen.' She asked if they wanted anything else. Embarrassed, they said no and left.

Outside, looking at the place from the car, they had to admit to each other that the windows were very nicely decorated. Reverse-painted from the inside, the one to the left had birds and fish seemingly floating or hanging in the glass. The one to the right was apparently of Christ in a dignified businessman's suit shaking hands with a sinner who bore an uncanny resemblance to himself.

I should perhaps tell how I came to be involved in all this. At the time the Executive Committee was switching to still another architect — from a Swede to a Norwegian — I had applied to be one of the Project Assistants. My application said that I had studied architecture and was currently engaged in the transport of services and materials. In fact I had studied architecture at the university, but for one term only. After that I bought an old double-decker bus and started a garbage run through two exclusive suburbs with a combined population of over 10,000. In the downstairs windows of the bus I pasted magazine pictures of faces and when the garbage started to get above the upstairs windows I would go away to dump it. It worked out very well — it looked like any other city bus going down the street and I never had one request for garbage to be returned. I emptied it in the hills above the city — so I think I told them too that I was a specialist in back-filling. But what I think really got me the job was that I told them truthfully I spoke two Scandinavian languages. They didn't ask which, but they were Danish and Swedish. And, as I've said, the new architect they hired was Norwegian.

At that time no one was concerned with such minutiae. Already the project was way over budget and everyone wanted it finished and quickly. For so long the Opera House externally appeared completed that people figured it ought just to be opened without further fuss or finance. That's why they hired me, I think, to assist the architect who didn't speak the language. And that too, I think, is why the Project Manager agreed with me that we accept Vic Mix's tender to paint the Opera House for $20,000. That is, they agreed with my argument that, if he botched it, the next man could just paint over what Vic had done. Since I couldn't speak Norwegian, the painting project was turned over to me.

I finally reached Vic by writing to the post office box number on his quotation. His response, on a postcard of the Taronga Park Zoo, disregarded all of my queries and instructions, nor did it acknowledge my description of the difficulty we had reaching him. It simply said: 'What do you want painted on it?' My response, agreed to by the Project Managers, was comparably terse: 'We want *paint* painted on it.' His next postcard, of Coolgardie, made more sense: 'What colour?' I told him we wanted something light, probably pastels, but certainly the soft colours of sand and sky. Another response, on stationery from a midwest US Hilton: 'When?' I checked its postmark and those of the rest of the correspondence and found it all to have come from Sydney. Intrigued, I wrote back at comparative length 'At your convenience, depending on your other jobs, but to be completed no later than Easter.' Vic responded in kind, via an inter-office memo from my own building: 'I'll see if I can fit it in. Don't worry.'

2

My office was on the other side of Sydney, but I frequently drove across just to look at the building. As the public knew, it was very exciting; and it was even more exciting for those intimately involved with it. However, time and money were running out and the City Fathers were impatient. As I drove by, day by day, despite little apparent progress, it looked more and more natural. With the passing of time it seemed progressively to have become at home with its surroundings, like great shells upon the shore or sails upon the bay. Seagulls hung lazily in the air, ferries drifted on the water, indiscriminate familiars to the House. But nothing seemed to be happening by way of its getting painted.

I often drove by the House at night. Once, returning

late, I noticed a light moving behind one of the great glass panes. I turned the car around and went back but when I got there the light was out and I could see no one. So I drove by the next night. I saw it again and went back. No one.

In the morning I called the night guard at his home. Yes, he said, there was a man out there painting. At first he would not let him in, but Vic had showed him our correspondence. The guard said Vic looked like a painter of a sort, but not one of the typical men working on the project. He was a big round bloke, with a beard and beret which made him look like a hairy acorn. He drove an old Indian motorcycle painted black with bones on it — ribs on the tank and a skull on the headlamp. But he was nice enough and quite industrious. It was just that he kept these odd hours, that was all. He worked hard, but always in the dark, so that you couldn't see how much work he'd done. Next morning I went by and looked carefully. I couldn't tell either.

When this had gone on for over a week I began to get very worried. I would have to call other tenders if the job weren't completed soon. The night guard said Vic was still at work but now had more people helping him. Like Vic, he said, they were an odd-looking lot; but, also like him, they were hard-working. He had only become aware of them by the vehicles arriving at night. At first there was a utility truck painted like a sea-going casket. Then there was a tricycle-like contraption with a great dunny built on the back (it even had a crescent cut into the door). Vic had told the guard that the one was designed for carrying the long-handled horizontal brushes, the other for the vertical ones. And he had introduced him to his two assistants, Mixmaster and Marijuanita. Though they didn't always seem to be the same people to the guard, they alway had the same kind of names: Mixwell and Mescalito and so on.

By now I was prepared to send Mr Mix a certified letter, cancelling his contract so that I could get him off the job and hire someone else. Just at that time I received a postcard from him. It was of the Opera House itself, the first such card I'd ever seen. Postmarked Sydney, it simply said: 'Finished.'

After work I drove over to the House but there was no

sign of him and no one in the parking lot. After some searching, I managed to find the guard on his rounds. He told me Mr Mix and his friends had left the night before, saying they would not be back. They were courteous as usual and cleaned up so well, the guard said, you couldn't tell they'd been there. I went home.

The next morning I was desperate. The job was supposed to be finished in a fortnight and didn't even seem to have been started. Mix would be paid and no one else contracted. I drove to the House to sit and think. I could always think better there. Perhaps I could come up with a solution before Monday.

In the early morning sun, gulls rising, ferries starting, I walked completely around the House and saw nothing unusual. Particularly I could find no sign of Mix and his colleagues having been there. I walked toward the water and sat on a piece of concrete. I was contemplating the House. The gulls, circling, seemed to be contemplating; the reflected people on the sweeping ferry seemed to be contemplating: *me*. Some gulls would hang, stoop, and then walk on the ground where they landed; others would land on the House itself or its windowsills.

As I watched, it seemed only half of them were moving. Some of the airborne ones were flying permanently in one place. The reflected ferry wasn't moving. I fixed my eye on one gull between me and the wall and walked steadily toward it. Thirty feet away I knew it wasn't moving at all. Only when I was right next to it did I realise it wasn't a gull but a painting of a gull on the outside wall of the House. The ferry was a painting on the window.

It was a regular *trompe l'oeil*. You could even see the people standing on the ferry deck. Everything was painted there on the window — everything outside the window. But at the same time I could see through the window. I was astounded, but I was frightened more: he had even painted the windows!

I ran to the other side of the building and managed to find the guard who let me in. I hurried through the building, back to the water side. Thank God, there was only the natural reflection of the room itself on the interior of the window. Or so I thought. Up close it was obvious that the glass was painted from this side too. Everything inside the room — the tables, chairs, hangings, everything. Another *trompe l'oeil.*

Vic Mix had co-ordinated the inner picture with the outer so from any one side you could not see the picture on the other. You could see through, or you could see where you were, inside looking out or outside looking in. I had to admit, though, he'd used pastels, natural colours of sand and sky.

I spent the rest of the day inspecting the House. It was the same everywhere. On each of the windows was painted the room looking out from the window. The outside windows were painted with the surroundings — the parking lot, the buildings, the streets, even the cars and people in the streets.

3

It was dark when I got home. Instead of eating, I sat down at the kitchen table with a bottle of scotch. I started doodling on a piece of paper and found myself drawing spheric sections on meridian curves of the same radius. By nine I was in bed, finishing the bottle. I dozed off. About midnight I jerked upright, wondering what it looked like at night.

I got up, dressed, and hurried to the car. When I got to the House the parking lot was deserted under the full moon. I parked and walked back to where I'd made my first discovery. A nocturnal gull was roosting at full speed on the side of the building. Looking closely, I could see that its head was the face of Jesus.

Looking toward the water, I saw the last ferry returning, lovers on the deck looking at the House in the moonlight. When I turned to the window, I saw the ferry painted there. The full moon, lovers on the deck. Each with the face of Jesus. I heard a noise from the parking lot at the other side of the House. As I walked around, I saw an old Graham leading an endless line of the oddest vehicles. The fire engine passed and I saw a sign on its side: 'VIC MIX AND THE TOPEKA CLIMAX ALL-TRUCK BAND.' It made no sense to me, though all the vehicles were trucks. Facing each other on its benches was an unlikely looking group. They had wild hair, clothing and bodies decorated with Day-Glo paint. I stood by the side of the building as the line passed from out of the street. Every face was identical.

Then I walked in their direction, anti-clockwise, against the traffic. Trucks and trucks passed: tip trucks, fuel trucks, tow trucks. As they did, I heard an indescribably agreeable music — motor groans, tyre whines, brake squeals, door thumps. The sounds mingled with the violet-indigo, purple-blue, green-yellow, orange-red, shining, spinning, flashing lights throughout the air.

It was a *son et lumière*, gathering speed. An alto calliope floated by, little puffs of pastel smoke punctuating the indefinite night. A bass cement truck, gliding lightly, was overspilling sweets from out its drum. A bitumen-spreader, a tenor in first gear, spread a living blanket of pillules that hopped about like jumping beans. Finally a pump engine, contralto and soprano, contrapuntally spewed forth pinkish jets that frothed into a mist that choked with ecstasy the dark night air.

They weaved through one another, became a double row. The music took on syncopation, the cyclic dance turned epicyclic. Then they stopped — the sky sagging like a great air-supported tent when the pressure drops. The moon folded in the middle, became a heart.

I had circumnavigated and was between the water and the House. The trucks had all turned left to face the centre. All but one, a flat-bed with a carbon arc lamp on its platform and a ramp at the back. It stopped and switched on its lamp and its beam of light began to rotate slowly overhead. The wrinkles of the night smoothed out, the sky billowed to a hemisphere. The stars shook twice and fixed themselves.

From the other direction an old hearse came hurtling at terrific speed, echoing a terrible groan. As I turned the curve its rear exploded and a motorcycle catapulted out the back heading the opposite way. When the motorcycle turned the other curve I saw the beret and box number on the licence plate.

Its roar became a drone, then a sob on the opposite side, and then a roar again. When it came in sight I could see the beard but not the face. It shot up the back of the flat-bed, inside the walls defined by the carbon arc beam in the night. Like a marble in a cone, it began to rise. Faster, higher, smaller. Smaller still. And then the light went out.

4

When I woke on Sunday morning I was stretched out beside my car. My body felt something my head could not remember. I walked all around the House and found it precisely as before. Inside too. I went home to bed.

On Monday morning I feared I would have to do a lot of explaining. However, when I got to work I found they'd just fired the Norwegian architect. So I was able to spend the day quietly arranging to have the House repainted and its windows replaced. I got a low quotation on both. By now everyone knew the financial plight of the project and quoted realistically. Besides, the glazier would get to keep the huge panes he replaced.

On Tuesday I was fired too. I guess they thought they no longer needed an architect who spoke a majority of the Scandinavian languages. I drove home wondering what the painters and glaziers would think when they saw the gulls and ferries. It occurred to me then that I had never met the architect.

On Wednesday, with nothing to do, I drove by the parlour, but it had been closed. They were setting up a do-it-yourself shop. I drove by the House and saw it there in soft pastels of sand, and sky, and air. Then I went by the office to pick up my mail. One letter was from Topeka, Kansas, USA. It only said, '. . . *because it takes me so long to find the bleedin' matches*'.

Elizabeth Jolley
FROM *FOXYBABY*

Alma Porch thought, with longing, of the fine fragrance of bacon and waited for her students. It was strange to feel so weak at the beginning of the day. She attributed this weak feeling to the lack of a proper breakfast. She was not remotely interested in lettuce or cereals.

Anna, occupied with her secret sorrow, ignoring her surroundings, still stood at the edge of the veranda. The thin children continued to chase each other.

'Good morning, Miss Porch, KFB.' Christobel folded up in front of Miss Porch.

'KFB? KFB?' Miss Porch was bewildered.

'Oh sorry,' Christobel laughed, 'we thought of the abbreviation, it's knees full-bend, remember? Miss Peycroft wants us to use the exercise as a greeting instead of saying "good morning". Remember?'

'Ah yes, of course.' Miss Porch, with two swollen knees, was unable to do more than stiffly bend her head forward.

'Is this all you have written?' Christobel asked.

'What d'you mean?'

'I mean where you've got the marker in your folder, is that as much as you've written?' Christobel's eyes, set wide-apart in her childish pink-and-white face, looked earnestly at Miss Porch. Standing very close to Miss Porch she gave the red marker a tweak.

'Heavens no!' Miss Porch, understanding, did not want to reveal that the question annoyed her. 'This is just for today's class. Don't pull the marker out, please.'

'Is it published?'

'Is what published.'

'That. Is that published?'

'No, not yet.' Miss Porch tried to look past Christobel's large good-natured face to see who else was approaching.

'I started writing some novels,' Christobel confided, 'years ago when I was in year ten. I've got heaps of material. I'm going to be a novelist. Mummy said I should ask you to recommend some publishers.' She turned her own notebook over. 'Oh!' she said, 'I've brought down the wrong book. I'll go up and get the other, don't start without me please.'

'What a delicious girl that is.' Mrs Viggars was beside Miss Porch who recognised the voice from the flower-bed conversation the evening before. 'I said to Rennett, "What a delicious girl," but Rennett's in a bit of a huff this morning. Oomph. Hasn't slept well.' Mrs Viggars laughed. 'There's a lot going on, isn't there.'

'Yes.' Miss Porch, with her back to the house, surveyed the activity in the courtyard. The weavers had already nailed up a screen of chicken wire at the side of the barn and were busily threading dry grasses, leaves and sticks through it, standing back to admire from time to time with little excited exclamations of delight.

In the double doorway of the shed the sculptors were gathered in a half-circle of reverence listening to Vladimir Lefftov the defected Russian Scrap Iron and Pop Art Sculptor. Miss Porch could hear Vladimir, whose quaint English was attractive, telling them that, like Mussorgsky, he wanted his characters to speak on the stage as they would in real life yet to make a performance which was artistic. The sculpting, he said, should be a mixture of real life, a cry from the soul of a real person but with the weight of Thought and the beauty of Art. Miss Porch felt she would like to be part of this; she wished to be not a tutor but a participant. She felt she would like to handle something from the heap at the side of the shed and make from it something which could reveal more than its immediate appearance of being ugly, spoiled and discarded.

The sculptors disappeared inside the shed and Miss Porch heard Vladimir's music, 'A Night on the Bald

Mountain', she thought she recognised it. She could hear the hammer strokes and wished to be able to watch Vladimir's initial demonstration. She waited for her students and for Miss Peycroft.

Miss Peycroft's voice came clearly, a dangerous contralto, through the kitchen window beside which Miss Porch had taken up her position.

'Miles,' Miss Peycroft was saying, 'I see that you have confiscated the mirrors again. Please see that they are put back in the rooms at once.'

'Fifty-seven mirrors is fifty-seven mirrors, Miss.' It was obviously a repeated conversation.

'Undoubtedly, Miles,' Miss Peycroft said, 'but kindly replace all the unsold ones immediately. And Miles, before you go, I must have a word about that dreadful sermon. Whatever possessed you! It was perfectly in order for you to spout from *Proverbs*:

Who can find a virtuous woman?
For her price is above rubies
The heart of her husband doth safely trust in her . . .

but to say all those commonplace and disgusting things and to repeat that crude joke in that language was, how shall I put it, quite beyond the pale. And what did your opinion about Women's Prisons have to do with any of it? If I hear you say once more that the women's prison is too small and that more women, especially the middle-aged and elderly, should be locked up — I'll — never mind what I'll do. I will just remind you once more that if transport was available most of the students would be leaving today. How could you, Miles! We could have lost this whole School before it got off the ground. And why — going back to the sermon, if you can call it that, how could you bring it all to the subjective in the way that you did by singing and I repeat singing, "Mrs Miles, she did not buy a vineyard, Mrs Miles, she did not buy a vineyard" *ad infinitum*, that's my phrase, I do not expect you to understand it. I must remind you that Mrs Miles has not yet bought this house.'

Miss Porch, hearing Miss Peycroft's voice break with indignation, moved away from the open window. A group of students, including Mrs Castle, Christobel and Mrs Viggars, were waiting. Miss Peycroft came out of the kitchen door unruffled except for a reddening of her eager nose. Miss Porch had hardly time to ponder on the thought, the possibility of Mrs Miles becoming the owner of Trinity College, of the House. Perhaps the House would become disreputable, a place of low repute and Mrs Miles a Madam. But who, Miss Porch wondered, would visit the House so far away from . . .

'Gratters! Josephine, mother and I want to say how much we enjoyed your opening lecture.' Miss Porch's ramblings were interrupted by the ex-teacher of gymnastics, Miss Crisp. Mrs Crisp, leaning on Miss Crisp's reliable arm, took her place in the semi-circle of hopeful students.

'Oh thank you, Yvonne,' Miss Peycroft said, 'it was nothing really. I simply used some notes from the old school days, Lower Third. Remember when we did Hedgerow Research, Seed Dispersal and Sanitary Landfill? Fascinating! So glad you enjoyed my little rehash. Now! Knees Full-Bend, Class. Down and Up and Down and Up. Not too far the first time, Mrs Crisp and Mrs Viggars. Gently! Gently! Down and Up and Down and Up. All set, Miss Porch? For the breakdown? For the breakdown of the scenes? The Foxybaby Treatment? We call it a Treatment,' she explained to the students who were regaining their balance as gracefully as possible.

'All set,' Miss Porch said unwillingly. She had not supposed that Miss Peycroft would be present. The whole idea of her class was, it seemed, slipping out of her hands. She would have to do her best to ignore Miss Peycroft if ignoring was possible.

Mrs Viggars, wearing white flared slacks and a portly blue blazer, was delighted to be cast as Doctor Steadman. 'I've brought my boots,' she said, 'you never know in advance what you're going to be asked to do.' Her heavy jowls quivered and her eyes behind the thick-lensed spectacles bulged. 'I'll just trot off and get my boots.' Her growling voice betrayed her pleasure.

She returned quickly with the immaculate trouser legs folded and pushed into the tops of the boots.

'Well, Rennett,' she said, rubbing her hands together, 'have you been cast yet? Oh I see you're to be a prison wardress, a screw it's called or rather a screwess I suppose you'd say, eh? What? Oomph?'

Anna showed no emotion at being asked to play Sandy, Steadman's daughter, though Miss Porch noticed that the pale skin of her neck and throat flushed slightly. It was pleasing too to notice an area of roughness and a few spots about the chin. A lip sore, she thought, would have been acceptable, but she was pleased with Anna's hair. Beneath an apparent sheen of a greenish colour on the top of the head, the hair underneath was sun-dried, pale with traces of old dye and had the stringlike quality of the hair of a sick person. Her feet too were thin with revealingly uncertain bones. Timid feet, Miss Porch thought with increasing pleasure. The girl's knuckles too, they whitened as she clenched her fist; nervous and irritable, Miss Porch hoped. 'Excellent!' Miss Porch said to herself. She felt there was a blossoming of the right kind of ugliness necessary for the part of Sandy. She glanced quickly at the top page of her notes. The file was heavy on her arm. She knew that her own bones were frail.

'We must,' Miss Peycroft announced in her loud voice, 'accept and acknowledge the truth of limitation and prepare to be condemned. We must dismiss,' she continued, 'what we feel to be sparse provision and have confidence. Thank you.'

The courtyard was freshly watered. The drama class waited for the treatment.

'All ready to start the breakdown of the storyline?' Miss Peycroft asked. Miss Porch nodded.

Rock music with a heavy disco beat pounded from the kitchen.

'Mrs Viggars,' Miss Porch said, faith in her own voice fading as she tried to raise her voice. It was as if she heard her own voice in some sort of dream from which she might wake at any moment. 'Mrs Viggars, you will speak your lines in first-person interior monologue. Here is your copy of the script . . .'

'Excuse me! I am not quite certain,' Jonquil Castle interrupted breathlessly, having been upstairs to change from her little lemon silk into the chocolate cotton, it being more suitable for the part of the nursing sister. 'I'm not quite clear,' she said, 'about first-person interior monologue. Is it the same as rivers of conscience?' With her head charmingly bobbing, tilted to one side and fluttering her carefully tinted eyelids she smiled at Miss Porch and at the assembled group.

'Stream of consciousness,' Miss Porch said. 'No, it is not the same thing at all. A discussion now,' she turned to Miss Peycroft, 'would hold things up terribly. I think,' she said, trying to sound firm, 'we must try to get started.'

'Yes of course. Rather!' Miss Peycroft frowned slightly and looked thoughtful. 'We should be held up till lunch time,' she said.

'Mrs Viggars,' Miss Porch said, ignoring Mrs Castle, 'as Dr Steadman . . .'

'Yes, Mrs Viggars' — Miss Peycroft stepped forward briskly. 'You are the lead. You are Dr Walter Steadman, an eminent professor and a scholar, burdened with one of the heaviest problems life can offer.'

Mrs Viggars nodded, puffing her good-natured flabby cheeks and her solid breast.

'As you walk,' Miss Peycroft continued, 'show in your demeanour that you are bearing something unbearable.' Miss Porch was about to explain more to Mrs Viggars but, before she could say anything, Miss Peycroft took up a hurricane lamp rented at enormous cost by Miss Porch from Miles and gave it to Miss Paisley. 'Wave this to and fro,' she said, 'this will indicate the flashing lights of the disco joint, I know it's only one colour but . . .'

Mrs Viggars, holding her script high in front of her face, paced towards the kitchen window. The other students stood in an obedient semi-circle watching.

'Foxybaby Treatment,' Miss Peycroft said, 'Foxybaby beat one, beat two, beat three. Take one, okay! "That's my daughter," that's where you start, okay! Okay!'

'That's my daughter.' Mrs Viggars cleared her throat and continued, 'that's my daughter in there with all those people. She's dancing in there. She's been dancing for hours, she's almost naked. All of them — naked — dancing non-stop, practically naked.'

'The flashing lights, blue and green, red and orange are all a part of the dance,' Miss Porch, trying not to be self-conscious, read aloud, 'the music has a heavy beat. It throbs and pulses. It screams and moans and beats . . .'

'Just a moment!' Miss Peycroft interrupted, 'turn the volume up in there please,' she called towards the kitchen, 'turn it up!' She turned to Miss Porch. 'Viggars, Steadman next?' she asked. Miss Porch nodded. 'Okay, Steadman,' Miss Peycroft said, 'okay, Steadman, your lines. Give them all you've got!'

'This music,' Mrs Viggars said, 'just now, this music is everything to her. She doesn't know that I'm here. I'll wait. I'll wait for her all night if I have to. She is completely given up to the dance.'

'Turns from the window,' Miss Porch said in a low voice, 'pauses — and now keep going with the first-person interior monologue.'

'Perhaps,' Mrs Viggars gave her pages a brisk shake, 'perhaps,' she said, 'we looked forward to the birth of the child with too much hope. Perhaps I was too hopeful. It's impossible to know what she hoped. I've always known that it is wrong to pin hopes on to a child but this is what people do. In my life this is the second time . . .

'No one in this little town recognises me in spite of my work and my television programmes. I am utterly alone and unknown. No one, not one friend knows that at this moment I'm standing outside this cheap noisy cafe in this dirty street.

She doesn't know that I'm here. She thinks, if she thinks at all, that I'm in that empty restaurant where she left me.

'We haven't been here long, two days. Perhaps I expected too much. She, when she spoke in one of her better moments, seemed to think that the holiday would do her good. I think I hoped for a miracle. Perhaps I am still hoping.

'During the journey I longed to tell her how much I loved her. Her baby too, I love him. He's ill with her illness. I couldn't find the right words. Any words I thought of were pompous or self-conscious. Perhaps, in reality, it has always been like that with me ...'

'Fade out,' Miss Porch said, 'fade in, continue, Viggars. You cut to the scene in the car now. Pause and continue.'

'The shadows lengthen across the paddocks, it is nearly dark,' Mrs Viggars read, 'we still have a long way to travel. The baby is unusually tranquil, sleeping in his cradle in the back of the car ...'

'A little more emphatic, Steadman, please.' Miss Porch, surprised at herself, was animated. She waved her papers. 'Go back to — "I longed to tell her ..." Do that bit again.'

Mrs Viggars nodded and, clearing her throat, read, 'I longed to tell her how much I loved her ...'

'Good! Goo-ood!' Miss Porch encouraged. Mrs Viggars smiled over the top of her script as she read on.

'Fade out, Steadman. Bring up Sandy,' Miss Porch said, 'starting with "My baby". Anna, you're in the car ... Steadman has looked back. Flashback to "My baby".'

'My baby.' Anna's thin fingers rustled like dry feathers on her sheets of manuscript. 'My baby. My baby's rotten like me. Even his mouth. He can't suck. The pain's awful. I never thought it would be like this. I wanted him born and now it feels like I don't want him. And this bloody journey, it's like it's never going to end. It's getting dark and we're not anywhere.

'"Look at the cows. Look at the freesias," He says. He's always on about something. How can I look at anything? He parrots on and on.

'I really thought everything would come right when I got

my baby. Like Hell! Shit! I feel cold. Cold all the way inside I'm cold. I want to be warm. I'm cold. Cold. Cold.

'My hair! It's one goddam mess. I hate my hair! "Stop scratching," He tells me. "Stop scratching, there's a good girl." He says it like I was a little girl again. His little girl, that's what he calls me. I can't be that again; never ever. I'm no one's. "There's sure to be a hairdressing shop," He says. Big deal! Hairdresser in this dump, this goddam place, a shithouse paddock. That's all it is.'

'Good,' Miss Porch said in a low voice. 'Steadman, your next line.'

Mrs Viggars cleared her throat, smiled quickly at Miss Porch and spoke: '"Wait till we reach the town," I want to tell her, *There is a town,* I want to console her with these lines, *There is a town by the rocks where the sea meets another sea*, but how can she be comforted by Sophocles? Instead I tell her that it's better to wait to have her hair done, "not too soon after childbirth," I say. My voice is too emotional, I know that my voice gives me away.

'Her hair is a knotted mass. I can't help my feelings of horror about the state of her skin. Her mouth is hidden in sores, infected eruptions. I keep hoping that the holiday will bring about a miracle . . .'

'Cut!' Miss Porch said. 'Excellent! Thank you, Steadman, Mrs Viggars.'

The music was suddenly louder.

'When's this noise leaving my kitching?' Mrs Miles, resplendent in new black satin, marched into the courtyard carrying the transistor. 'I can't hear myself think in there,' she said to Miss Porch, 'I can't hear nothing of what's in my own head. It's past mawnin teas, I can't keep on the boil all day and I don't care to be stared at in me own kitching.'

'Oh sorry,' Miss Porch said, 'thank you, Mrs Miles.' She took the transistor and switched it off. 'We'll have a ten-minute break,' she said to the students, 'and then straight back here. Right? For the next *tableau vivant,* Sandy — that's you, Anna — will need to slip from the cafe to the bench over there. This will be for the scene set in the hospital ward. I shall read in the third person present tense for the treatment. Ten minutes break then.' Miss Porch felt her trembling would be noticed; she seemed to shake from head to foot.

'How d'you do it! It's great!' A little group surrounded Mrs Viggars.

'Oh, Mrs Viggars, let me get your tea for you!' Christobel was flushed with excitement.

Mrs Viggars seemed perplexed. She held her paper beaker of black tea as if she did not understand why it was in her hand.

Miss Porch noticed, with shy pleasure, that Anna was paler and that her hair was positively awful. She seemed to have stopped staring into a vague distance and she took absolutely no notice of her two little boys.

'I fear your Mussorgsky will drown our cello!' Miss Porch, surprised at her own boldness, called across the yard to Vladimir who was waving the steaming stinkwort to and fro in the doorway of the barn. 'I turn down,' he called in reply. 'Too hot!' he tapped the beaker. His smile, in her direction, made Miss Porch feel quite pretty.

'On location!' she raised a whistle to her lips. 'Come along, Drama!' She blew the whistle and the students came hurrying back from all over the courtyard.

Miles, doffing his cap, limped round the broken edge of the orchard wall.

'Oh goody, Miles! You've got the video all set up.' Miss Peycroft, with her cello, took her place on a chair near Miss Porch.

'I must just tell you, Alma,' she said in a low voice, 'don't expect too much this morning. Anna's a perfect zombie today. I'm told she's stuffed herself with Valium. She's not exactly with us —'

Miss Porch, with a suitable expression of understanding, nodded. 'Steadman,' she said, 'Steadman — Mrs Viggars,' she looked from her page across to Mrs Viggars. 'Anna,' she said, 'you are Sandy and and Mrs Castle, you will be the nursing sister . . .'

'Excuse me one moment, if I may.' Miss Peycroft jumped up. 'Miss Porch will read and the characters will mime the action. Miss Porch and I would like you,' she said, 'to observe the effect of mime on the human individual. We shall discuss the performance which will be on video this evening. Please, Miss Porch, do go on, sorry for the interruption.'

'Miss Rennett and Miss Harrow,' Miss Porch said, trying to form a picture in anticipation of the effect of mime on the human individual. She began, in her mind, to see a large circle of people of various shapes and sizes (the individual) walking slowly round and round, each person with a hand delicately placed (mime) on the shoulder of the person in front. 'Miss Rennett and Miss Harrow,' she said again, 'please will you take up your positions on the other side of the wire fence. That's right. I know it is a poultry pen but for the prison scene the effect will be admirable.'

'One more little thing.' Miss Peycroft sprang up once more, the cello perilously balanced. 'For the purpose of the *tableau vivant'* — she surveyed the group of students — 'if you like to split up you may also take part in the mime and the camera will include some long shots which should give a mirror-like effect of the action. I hope this idea appeals?' She looked at Miss Porch with her eyebrows raised.

'Oh quite, thank you,' Miss Porch replied. 'Right!' she said, 'music, please.'

Helen Garner

THE LIFE OF ART

My friend and I went walking the dog in the cemetery. It was a Melbourne autumn: mild breezes, soft air, gentle sun. The dog trotted in front of us between the graves. I had a pair of scissors in my pocket in case we came across a rose bush on a forgotten tomb.

'I don't like roses,' said my friend. 'I despise them for having thorns.'

The dog entered a patch of ivy and posed there. We pranced past the Elvis Presley memorial.

'What would you like to have written on your grave,' said my friend, 'as a tribute?'

I thought for a long time. Then I said, '*Owner of two hundred pairs of boots.*'

When we had recovered, my friend pointed out a headstone which said, *She lived only for others*. 'Poor thing,' said my friend. 'On *my* grave I want you to write, *She lived only for herself*.'

We went stumbling along the overgrown paths.

My friend and I had known each other for twenty years, but we had never lived in the same house. She came back from Europe at the perfect moment to take over a room in the house I rented. It became empty because the man — but that's another story.

My friend has certain beliefs which I have always secretly categorised as *batty*. Sometimes I have thought, 'My friend is what used to be called "a dizzy dame".' My friend believes in reincarnation: not that this in itself is unacceptable to me. Sometimes she would write me long letters from wherever she was in the world, letters in her lovely, graceful, sweeping hand, full of tales from one or other of her previous lives, tales to explain her psychological make-up and behaviour in her present incarnation. My eye would fly along the lines, sped by embarrassment.

My friend is a painter.

When I first met my friend she was engaged. She was wearing an antique sapphire ring and Italian boots. Next time I saw her, in Myer's, her hand was bare. I never asked. We were students then. We went dancing in a club in South Yarra. The boys in the band were students too. We fancied them, but at twenty-two we felt ourselves to be older women, already fading, almost predatory. We read *The Roman Spring of Mrs Stone*. This was in 1965; before feminism.

My friend came off the plane with her suitcase. 'Have you ever noticed,' she said, 'how Australian men, even in their forties, dress like small boys? They wear shorts and thongs and little stripey T-shirts.'

A cat was asleep under a bush in our backyard each morning when we opened the door. We took him in. My friend and I fought over whose lap he would lie in while we watched TV.

My friend is tone deaf. But she once sang 'Blue Moon', verses and chorus, in a talking, tuneless voice in the back of a car going up the Punt Road hill and down again and over the river, travelling north; and she did not care.

My friend lived as a student in a house near the university. Her bed was right under the window in the front room downstairs. One afternoon her father came to visit. He tapped on the door. When no one answered he looked through the window. What he saw caused him to stagger back into the fence. It was a kind of heart attack, my friend said.

My friend went walking in the afternoons near our house. She came out of lanes behind armfuls of greenery. She found vases in my dusty cupboards. The arrangements she made with the leaves were stylish and generous-handed.

Before either of us married, I went to my friend's house to help her paint the bathroom. The paint was orange, and so was the cotton dress I was wearing. She laughed because all she could see of me when I stood in the bathroom were my limbs and my head. Later, when it got dark, we sat at her kitchen table and she rolled a joint. It was the first dope I had ever seen or smoked. I was afraid that a detective might look through the kitchen window. I could not understand why my friend did not pull the curtain across. We walked up to Genevieve in the warm night and ate two bowls of spaghetti. It seemed to me that I could feel every strand.

My friend's father died when she was in a distant country.

'So now,' she said to me, 'I know what grief is.'

'What is it?' I said.

'Sometimes,' said my friend, 'it is what you expect. And sometimes it is nothing more than bad temper.'

When my friend's father died, his affairs were not in order and he had no money.

My friend was the first person I ever saw break the taboo against wearing striped and floral patterns together. She stood on the steps of the Shrine of Remembrance and held a black umbrella over her head. This was in the 1960s.

My friend came back from Europe and found a job. On the days when she was not painting theatre sets for money she went to her cold and dirty studio in the city and painted for the other thing, whatever that is. She wore cheap shoes and pinned her hair into a roll on her neck.

My friend babysat, as a student, for a well-known woman in her forties who worked at night.

'What is she like?' I said.

'She took me upstairs,' said my friend, 'and showed me her bedroom. It was full of flowers. We stood at the door looking in. She said, "Sex is not a problem for me."'

When the person ... the man whose room my friend had taken came to dinner, my friend and he would talk for hours after everyone else had left the table about different modes of perception and understanding. My friend spoke slowly, in long, convoluted sentences and mixed metaphors, and often laughed. The man, a scientist, spoke in a light, rapid voice, but he sat still. They seemed to listen to each other.

'I don't mean a god in the Christian sense,' said my friend.

'It is egotism,' said the man, 'that makes people want their lives to have meaning beyond themselves.'

My friend and I worked one summer in the men's underwear department of a big store in Footscray. We wore our little cotton dresses, our blue sandals. We were happy there, selling, wrapping, running up and down the ladder, dinging the register, going to the park for lunch with the boys from the shop. *I* was happy. The youngest boy looked at us and sighed and said, 'I don't know which one of youse I love the most.' One day my friend was serving a thin-faced woman at the specials box. There was a cry. I looked up. My friend was dashing for the door. She was sobbing. We all stood still, in attitudes of drama. The woman spread her hands. She spoke to the frozen shop at large.

'I never said a thing,' she said. 'It's got nothing to do with *me*.'

I left my customer and ran after my friend. She was halfway down the street, looking in a shop window. She had stopped crying. She began to tell me about . . . but it doesn't matter now. This was in the 1960s; before feminism.

My friend came home from her studio some nights in a calm bliss. 'What we need,' she said, 'are those moments of abandon, when the real stuff runs down our arm without obstruction.'

My friend cut lemons into chunks and dropped them into the water jug when there was no money for wine.

My friend came out of the surgery. I ran to take her arm but she pushed past me and bent over the gutter. I gave her my hanky. Through the open sides of the tram the summer wind blew freely. We stood up and held on to the leather straps. 'I can't sit down,' said my friend. 'He put a great bolt of gauze up me.' This was in the 1960s; before feminism. The tram rolled past the deep gardens. My friend was smiling.

My friend and her husband came to visit me and my husband. We heard their car and looked out the upstairs window. We could hear his voice haranguing her, and hers raised in sobs and wails. I ran down to open the door. They were standing on the mat, looking ordinary. We went to Royal Park and flew a kite that her husband had made. The nickname he had for her was one he had picked up from her father. They both loved her, of course. This was in the 1960s.

My friend was lonely.

My friend sold some of her paintings. I went to look at them in her studio before they were taken away. The smell of the oil paint was a shock to me: a smell I would have thought of as masculine. This was in the 1980s; after feminism. The paintings were big. I did not 'understand' them; but then again perhaps I did, for they made me feel like fainting, her weird plants and creatures streaming back towards a source of irresistible yellow light.

'When happiness comes,' said my friend, 'it's so thick and smooth and uneventful, it's like nothing at all.'

My friend picked up a fresh chicken at the market. 'Oh,' she said. 'Feel this.' I took it from her. Its flesh was pimpled and tender, and moved on its bones like the flesh of a very young baby.

I went into my friend's room while she was out. On the wall was stuck a sheet of paper on which she had written: 'Henry James to a friend in trouble: "throw yourself on the *alternative* life . . . which is what I mean by the life of art, and which religiously invoked and handsomely understood, je vous le garantis, never fails the sincere invoker — sees him through everything, and reveals to him the secrets of and for doing so."'

I was sick. My friend served me pretty snacks at sensitive intervals. I sat up on my pillows and strummed softly the five chords I had learnt on my ukulele. My friend sat on the edge of a chair, with her bony hands folded round a cup, and talked. She uttered great streams of words. Her gaze skimmed my shoulder and vanished into the clouds outside the window. She was like a machine made to talk on and on forever. She talked about how much money she would have to spend on paint and stretchers, about the lightness, the optimism, the femaleness of her work, about what she was going to paint next, about how much tougher and more violent her pictures would have to be in order to attract proper attention from critics, about what the men in her field were doing now, about how she must find this out before she began her next lot of pictures.

'Listen,' I said. 'You don't have to think about any of that. Your work is *terrific.'*

'My work is terrific,' said my friend on a high note, 'but *I'm not.*' Her mouth fell down her chin and opened. She began to sob. 'I'm forty,' said my friend, 'and I've got *no money.*'

I played the chords G, A and C.

'I'm lonely,' said my friend. Tears were running down her cheeks. Her mouth was too low in her face. 'I want a man.'

'You could have one,' I said.

'I don't want just any man,' said my friend. 'And I don't want a boy. I want a man who's not going to think my ideas are crazy. I want a man who'll see the part of me that no one ever sees. I want a man who'll look after me and love me. I want a grown-up.'

I thought, If I could play better, I could turn what she has just said into a song.

'Women like us,' I said to my friend, 'don't have men like that. Why should *you* expect to find a man like that?'

'Why shouldn't I?' said my friend.

'Because men won't do those things for women like us. We've done something to ourselves so that men won't do it.

Well — there are men who will. But we despise them.'

My friend stopped crying.

I played the ukulele. My friend drank from the cup.